THE GOSPEL,
THE SPIRIT, THE CHURCH

The Gospel, the Spirit, the Church

Keswick Ministry from John Stott, Dick Lucas, Ken Prior, Gilbert Kirby and others

Edited from transcripts by David Porter

STL Books

P.O. Box 48, Bromley, Kent, England

Keswick Convention Council, England

© 1978 The Keswick Convention Council.

STL Books are published by Send the Light Trust, 9 London Road, Bromley, Kent, England.

Cover photograph by Canon K. W. Coates.

All Rights Reserved. No part of this publication may be reproduced, stored in a retrieval system, or transmitted, in any form or by any means, electronic, mechanical, photocopying, recording or otherwise without the prior permission of the Keswick Convention Council.

ISBN 0 903843 02 1

Printed by Hunt Barnard Printing Ltd., Aylesbury, Bucks.

CONTENTS

The Addresses

INTRODUCTION

by Canon A. S. Neech,
(Chairman of the Keswick Convention
Council)

In British Christian circles there can be few place-names better known than Keswick. For more than a hundred years thousands of people have attended the annual Conventions held in the little town of that name in the English Lake District. And, over the years, in dozens of other places in the U.K. and in a still growing number of overseas countries, other Conventions calling themselves 'Keswick' have been established. They all bear witness to the fact that God really does speak through the Bible and that lives are changed in response to that Word.

This book contains part of what was preached at the English Keswick in 1978. Each year there are two weeks of Conventions. The first offers a very full programme with several meetings every day. The second, called 'Holiday Week' is geared mainly for families and has far fewer meetings arranged. In each week the Bible Readings are a main feature of the Conventions. It was felt therefore that most of this little book should be devoted to them. The rest of the space available contains a selection of other addresses given. Some of these have been considerably compressed. For those who want to hear all the talks that were given, tape recordings are available on application to the Keswick Tapes Office, 13 Lismore Road, Eastbourne, East Sussex, England. See also the list of tapes from which this book was compiled, on page 192.

Keswick stands for the reverent, diligent, honest study of God's Word and for faithful obedience to its revealed truths. This is a soul-satisfying exercise always leading to a deeper commitment to God in a life of personal holiness and to His purpose in the world.

Rapt attention characterised the hearing of the talks you are now to read. Hundreds have spoken of the blessing they brought. May you too find them relevant and refreshing.

EDITOR'S INTRODUCTION

In his introduction, Canon Neech has indicated the very special place that Keswick holds in the hearts of those who attend the Convention or who share in it in other ways – such as reading books like this, which give the ministry a more permanent existence and a wider audience. A large part of my task as editor has been to attempt to preserve the 'feel' of the Convention – what it was like to be there, and how the addresses sounded as they were delivered by the speakers. This book is a record of an occasion.

It is a great deal more than that as well. It is a selection of biblical exposition and teaching, by speakers who were united in a common desire to eagerly study and faithfully expound Scripture. As a result God honoured the teaching as he always will honour the sober study of his word, and what you have in this book is a collection of addresses which are very relevant not only to the crowds who actually attended Keswick in 1978, but to all of us.

A remarkable unanimity of mind characterises the contributions. Often – and always unconsciously – speakers echoed each other's thoughts and extended each other's insights. Strands of teaching ran through the whole Convention, being taken up by different speakers in turn, and some of this is apparent even in this selection. And the speakers addressed themselves to vitally relevant topics. What does God want his Church to be like? What does he want it to do? And, in the contexts of church, family and work, what does it mean to be filled with the Spirit?

Working through these addresses in the process of editing them has been a privilege, and I have found the editing of this book – as I hope you will with the reading of it – a tremendously helpful and upbuilding experience. Of course much has had to be cut out. I have worked on the principle that careful pruning is better than wholesale paraphrase, and what is now printed is more or less the words that the speakers spoke. I have had, reluctantly, to cut out some good anecdotes. Most of the preliminary material, all the introductions, and all the closing prayers have had to go. I have reduced most Scripture references down to the most relevant fragments, so that it will be necessary to have an open Bible before you as you read if you are to get the most out of the addresses.

It was A. A. Milne who defended his dramatised version of Kenneth Grahame's *Wind in the Willows* by explaining that, if one *had* to have thumbprints on one's bread-and-butter, it was preferable that they were one's own. And certainly, if the addresses which I have listened to several times on tape and read through in transcript *have* to be edited, then (purely selfishly) I am glad to have had the task myself. Editing is inevitably rather a personal activity. The choice of what to leave out is, in the end, a personal one. And it is important that this book should be seen as a record of spoken addresses, rather than as material conceived for book publication and prepared by the authors with that in mind. They have all co-operated very graciously in this project, but they are busy men and have not been able to check and revise the edited version, although it has been read over on behalf of the Keswich Convention Council.

I hope that something of the spirit of the event itself and the teaching that was given will be apparent to you as you read this book.

THE BIBLE READINGS

GOSPEL AND CHURCH
Lessons from First Thessalonians
by the Rev. John Stott

1. Christian Evangelism; How the Gospel Spreads (1 Thessalonians 1)

In chapter 1, Paul refers to both the church (verses 1–4) and the Gospel (verses 5–10): the church of God, which the Gospel has created, and then the Gospel of God and how the church spreads it. First, then,

The church of God (verses 1–4)

It is really amazing to read Paul's beautiful and comprehensive description of the Thessalonian church. I remind you, it was only a few months old. Its members were new-born Christians, with the fresh bloom of conversion upon them. Both their convictions and standards were being tested by persecution. Now you'd think, wouldn't you, that it would be a very wobbly church? But no. Paul is confident about this church. He knows it's God's church in three ways.

1. *It is a community in God the Father and the Lord Jesus Christ.* Verse 1, 'Paul, Silas and Timothy to the church of the Thessalonians in God the Father and the

Lord Jesus Christ.' (Notice in passing the unselfconscious way in which Paul brackets God the Father and Jesus Christ together as the one source of the church's power. Already, within twenty years of the death and resurrection of Jesus! It's universally accepted. He doesn't need to argue it.) In his later letters Paul tended to describe the church the other way round, for example 'the church of God in Corinth'. And he could have put it like that here: the church of God in Thessalonica. But he reverses it. 'The church of the Thessalonians "in God".' Both were true. Every church has two homes, two habitats. It lives in God and it lives on earth, in the world. Why, do you think, did Paul decide to describe the church in Thessalonica in this particular way? Well, we can guess that he did it because he knew the insecurity they felt. He wanted to remind them that even if they were oppressed by men their security was in God. It is from him that every church derives its life and power; and so Paul wishes them grace and peace. We today can derive no greater blessings and desire no greater blessings for the church than God's peace, his *shalom*, through reconciliation with God and one another; and God's grace, his free and unmerited favour to bring about and sustain this peace.

So the church is a community in God the Father and in the Lord Jesus Christ, rooted in God, deriving its life and power from him.

2. *It is a community characterised by faith, hope and love.* Verses 2, 3: 'We give thanks . . . mention you . . . remember you.' Memory, thanksgiving and prayer belong together in a Christian's devotional life. Perhaps some of us who are getting middle-aged or elderly need to pray for the stimulation of our rotten memories! It's when we remember people, their names, faces and

situations, that we're stimulated to want to thank God for them and pray for them.

Now what Paul specially remembers about the Thessalonian church is what we usually call the three cardinal Christian graces or virtues; their faith, love and hope. They're indispensable characteristics of an authentically Christian life (we all know 1 Corinthians 13 where Paul elaborates them further). So let's test ourselves. Are we authentic Christians? It depends if we're characterised by faith and love and hope. A trustful commitment to God through Jesus Christ. Love for others both in the church and beyond it. And hope for the future, as we look for the coming, in great magnificence, of our Lord Jesus. Every Christian without exception is a believer, a lover, a hoper (not an optimist; optimism is hoping for the best without any grounds. Hope is quite different. It looks for the Lord's return and rests upon sure promises). So faith, love and hope are sure evidences of our regeneration by the Holy Spirit. Together they seem to turn us inside out, as they reorientate our whole life, so that we find ourselves drawn upwards to God in faith, outwards to other people in love, and onwards to the second coming of Christ in hope.

Paul lays emphasis on one more point about faith and hope and love. Each is productive. They sound very abstract, but they have concrete, practical results. Our *faith in God* leads to good works, without which faith is spurious. The Christian is no Little Johnny-Head-in-Air. Who says there is a dichotomy between Paul and James? They both say that faith leads to works. Our *love for people* leads to labour, the labour of love. If it doesn't, our love isn't real. It's sentimentality. And our *hope in Christ* leads to endurance as we wait for his coming in the face of persecution, otherwise we can't really be expectantly awaiting our Lord's return. The New International Version puts it very succinctly, following the Greek: 'Your work produced by faith, your labour prompted by love and your endurance inspired by hope in our Lord Jesus Christ.' Faith, hope and love, if they are authentic, are very productive in Christian living.

3. *The church is also a community loved and chosen by God.* Verse 4: '. . . we know, brethren, beloved by God, that he has chosen you.' Here is the teaching of the New Testament and the Old, that God has set his love on his people in eternity and chosen them. Thus the love of God and the election of God are joined invariably to one another in Scripture. We find it in Deuteronomy 7: 7, 8 where Moses says to Israel,

> It was not because you were more in number than any other nation that the Lord set his love upon you and chose you. No, the reason why he set his love upon you and chose you is that he loves you.

He loves you because he loves you. There is no explanation of the love of God except that love of God. And there is no explanation of the election of God except the love of God. 'And we know, brethren, beloved by God' – your election by God. He loved you. He chose you. Beyond that mystery we cannot penetrate.

However what is striking in verse 4 is not so much that Paul describes them as loved and chosen by God as that he says he knows their election. How could he possibly be so sure that these Thessalonian Christians belong to the elect people of God? Well, the context tells us. When the Gospel came to them it came to them not in word only but in power, so they received it. And it bore fruit in their lives, in a work of faith, and a labour of love, and an endurance of hope. It's because of that that he knew their election. It worked in their lives. When he preached the Gospel to them they responded to it and were transformed by it.

The doctrine of election, you see, can never be made an excuse either for giving up evangelism or for giving up the pursuit of holiness. On the contrary; it is precisely *by* evangelism that God's elect are discovered. It's precisely *by* holiness that they give evidence of their election, and it is only when people respond to the Gospel and grow in holiness that their secret election by God becomes apparent and visible to men.

Now what's the main thing we learn from all this? Well, I want to emphasis this. The main element in the church's identity is that it is the church of God. We need so badly to develop Paul's perspective. To him the church isn't a kind of religious club, united by a common interest. Still less is it a group of Paul's followers, united in their allegiance to him. It is *God's church*. A people chosen and loved by God in all eternity, rooted in God the Father and in the Lord Jesus Christ, drawing its life and power from him, and exhibiting this divine life in a faith that works, a love that labours and a hope that endures. And you and I, in our man-centred age, especially, I think, if we're pastors and leaders in the church, need to check ourselves by Paul's God-centredness. We need to learn to think of the church as a people whose primary relationship is neither to us, not to each other as fellow-members, not to the world that they are called to serve; but to God, on whose love they depend and from whom they derive their life and power. Only so can we be confident of the church's stability. And thank God for the church.

19

John Stott

The Gospel of God (verses 5–10)

From the church of God we turn to the Gospel of God. Paul, as we've seen, cannot think of one without the other. In these verses he sets out the progress of the Gospel in three clear stages.

1. *It 'came to you' (verse 5).* It didn't come by itself. It came because it was brought, by Paul and Silas and Timothy. Before they arrived in Thessalonica there wasn't a Christian church there. When they left, the church had been planted and taken root. The planting of the church is the direct result of the preaching of the Gospel. Paul describes how he proclaimed it.

He proclaimed it *in word*. The Gospel itself is a word. Paul calls it that in verse 6. It's the word of God, the word of the Lord. The Gospel has a specific content. And that content is to be found in Scripture. The Gospel can come to people only in words. Ah, but not in words only!

It came *in power*. By themselves, human words are weak and ineffective. People don't always hear them. If they hear them they don't always grasp them. If they grasp them, they don't always feel their impact. Words need to be confirmed by divine power. Otherwise they don't reach the minds and the consciences and the wills of the hearers. The Gospel came in words, and it came in power.

The Gospel came *with full conviction*. Power refers to the objective result of the preaching. Conviction refers to the subjective state of the preacher. He is sure of his message, sure of its truth and relevance, and so he is bold in its proclamation. And this assurance and this courage are precisely what so many modern preachers lack.

20

The Gospel was proclaimed *in the Holy Spirit*. I take this expression last because it seems to me that it belongs to all the other three. Truth, conviction and power all come from the Holy Spirit. It's he who illumines our minds, so that we formulate our message with clarity. It's he whose inward witness assures us of its truth, so that we proclaim it with conviction. It's he who carries it home with power, so that the hearers respond in penitence and faith. Three characteristics of all true preaching, all springing from the Holy Spirit.

Oh, that we had preachers of that calibre in our pulpits today! Men with a message, men with conviction, men of power and men of the Holy Spirit. 'Our Gospel came to you' – like that!

2. *'You received' it (verses 6, 7)*. That is, their hearts were opened by the Holy Spirit to understand and believe and obey the message. Again, four points.

You received it *in much affliction*. In Thessalonica there had been considerable opposition to the preaching of the word, to those who preached it and those who listened to it. But the Thessalonian Christians welcomed the Gospel, in the midst of opposition and in spite of it.

You received it *with joy, inspired by the Holy Spirit*. Don't miss this second reference to the Holy Spirit. The same Spirit worked at both ends – in the preacher and in the hearer. He always brings the two together. And there was joy, because joy is the fruit of the Spirit. Wherever the Gospel goes and people respond, there is joy. There's joy in heaven among the angels, and there's joy on earth among the people of God. So there was affliction and there was joy.

You became *imitators of us and of the Lord*. That is, in your experience of affliction and joy, and indeed in every other aspect of your Christian life, you followed

21

the example of us, Paul says, that is the apostles, and so of Christ whose apostles they were. To receive the word included that. It's not just to give an intellectual acquiescence in its truth. It is a complete transformation of life.

Lastly, you became *an example to all the believers.* For those who take Christ as their model become themselves models for others. Marvellous, isn't it? To see the beneficial effects of the Gospel in those who receive it Oh, it may mean opposition – it often has done. But it also involves inward joy through the Holy Spirit, the imitation of Christ and his apostles, in transformed and obedient lives, and the setting of an example to other believers.

3. *The word of the Lord sounded forth from you (verses 8–10).* The Greek word means to sound, to ring, to peal, to boom. It's used in the Greek version of the Old Testament of bells, zithers, trumpets and other loud noises. In the New Testament it's used of a 'noisy gong and clanging cymbal', and, in some manuscripts of Luke 21, of the roaring of the sea. So in either case, you see, whether Paul is likening Gospel preaching to a peal of bells or to the sound of a trumpet, it's a loud noise that that the Gospel made. It reverberated throughout Greece, through Northern Greece (Macedonia and Southern Greece (Achaia). And all over the country the noise echoed on and reverberated among the hills and the valleys of Greece. The Thessalonians simply hadn't been able to keep the good news to themselves! Besides, Thessalonica was a seaport and a capital city as well, so it was strategically placed. From that city the message of the Gospel spread far and fast, as the messengers carried it out of the city.

But there was something more than that, and it's

very important to see this. Verse 8: 'Not only has the voice of the Lord sounded forth from you' – that is, not only have you preached it and sent out messengers to preach it, but, your faith in God has gone forth everywhere – 'so that we need not say anything'!

I think it's a very, very important lesson to learn here about Christian evangelism. We live in a media-conscious generation. We know the power of the mass media. Consequently we want to use the media for evangelism, by print, by film, by radio, by television. And rightly so: we Christians should use every modern medium of communication available to us. But don't let us forget that there is another medium of communication even more effective. It's very simple indeed. It's spontaneous. It costs nothing. What is it? It's *holy gossip*. It's the excited transmission of the impact that the good news makes upon people. 'Do you know that so-and-so's a completely changed person?' 'Why, something's going on in Thessalonica – a new society is coming into being. Have you heard about it?' You see, the Gospel is spreading!

Now the result of all that gratuitous publicity was tremendous. 'We need not say anything.' Not only were the media redundant. The missionaries were redundant! The message was spreading without them and everybody seemed to know it already. Now mind you, I don't think Paul quite literally meant that he was no longer necessary. At least, he didn't apply for an indefinite furlough! He carried on preaching the Gospel, especially where Christ wasn't known. Nevertheless, we take his point. The good news was spreading spontaneously.

What exactly was the good news that was spreading from Thessalonica? Well, at the end of verse 8 Paul says it

23

was 'your faith in God'. That's what people were hearing about. But in the last two verses, 9 and 10, Paul gives a three part analysis of what he meant by their faith in God. And it's one of the fullest and most succinct descriptions anywhere in the New Testament of what is meant by conversion. Conversion, according to Paul, involves at least these three things: one, you turn to God from idols, two, you turn from idols in order to serve the living and true God, and three, you wait for his son from heaven. In those three verbs – turning, serving, waiting – you have an analysis of what the New Testament means by conversion.

Firstly *a decisive break with idols*. I think it would be difficult to exaggerate how radical is the change of allegiance that is implied. Idols are creatures, the work of men's hands, dead, false, many and visible; God is the creator of the universe and of all mankind, and he is living, true, one and invisible. A tribe's traditional idols have a tremendous hold upon the people's minds and their whole lives. For centuries the tribe has lived in superstitious dread and obsequious submission to them. The very thought of breaking away from the idols or from the spirits fills them with alarm because they're afraid that the idols or spirits will take revenge upon them. And the same is true in the West. Our more sophisticated idols, or God-substitutes, are equally powerful in men's lives. Think of a man or woman simply eaten up with ambition for power or fame or money. Or another obsessed with work, or another addicted to sex or alcohol. In each case it is an idolatry, because it demands a total allegiance. And idolater is a prisoner, an addict of his idol.

And then suddenly, completely, this person turns, from the idols that have controlled his life so far into a liberating experience of the living God. It is an encounter with Jesus Christ in which the spell of the idol is broken and the superior power of the living and true God is demonstrated, and people are amazed, and they are filled with awe, and they spread the news 'the idol's power is broken'.

Secondly, *an active service of God.* The claim to have turned from idols is manifestly bogus if it doesn't result in serving the God to whom we turn. We mustn't think of conversion in purely negative terms: we must think of it also in positive terms as the beginning of a new life of service. You turn from idols to the living and true God – to serve him. We could say that it is an exchange of one slavery for another, so long as we add immediately that the new slavery is a real liberation. Indeed, so total is true conversion that it involves a double liberation: firstly *from* the power of the idols to whom we previously bowed down, and then *into* the service of the true and living God, whom to serve is authentic, human freedom.

Thirdly, *a patient waiting for Christ.* To me it's very striking indeed that waiting and serving go together in the Christian life. Serving is active: waiting is passive. Serving is getting busy for Christ on earth. Waiting is looking for Christ to come from heaven. So this coupling, you see, of waiting and serving, expresses a very important recognition. On the one hand, however hard we work and serve there are limits to what we can achieve. We have to wait for Christ to come from heaven, and only then will he secure the final triumph of God's reign of justice and of peace. But on the other hand, although we must wait patiently for Christ to come, we have to work while we are waiting. So working, serving the true and living God, and waiting, belong together. And this combination will deliver us on the one hand from the presumption that we imagine that we can do everything, and from the pessimism that imagines that we can do nothing. And of the coming of God's own son from heaven, for which we wait, we can be absolutely sure, because (verse 10) God has raised him from the dead.

Now I think we're in a position to summarise the report about the Thessalonians which was being disseminated throughout Greece and beyond. And so we can understand the essentials of Christian conversion. The turning from idols, the serving of the living God, and the waiting for Christ. We're given a model of Christian conversion. It's not only comprehensive, it's actually invariable. It's always the same. Of course there will be different forms which one's service of the living God will take. But always the break with the past will be decisive, the experience of service will be liberating, and the look for the future will be expectant. And without this turning, this serving and this waiting, one can scarcely claim to have been converted.

I want us to try to grasp the indispensible relationship between the church and the Gospel. We must not – indeed we cannot – separate the two. Every true church is a Gospel church and we need more Gospel churches in the world today. So I finish with these two points.

1. *The church that receives the Gospel must pass it on.* Don't you agree with me? Nothing really is more impressive in chapter one than the sequence: it came to you, you received it, it sounded forth from you. Every local church is to be a sounding board for the Gospel. God's simple plan for the spread of the Gospel is absolutely plain. The church that receives it, sounds it forth.

And if the church had been faithful to God's purpose the world would long since have been evangelised.

2. *The church that passes it on must embody it.* Because we saw, didn't we, that the Thessalonians passed it on not only by the word of the Lord sounding forth verbally, but by news of their conversion. This holy gossip about what had happened to them was spreading abroad. It was exciting. People came to Thessalonica to have a look for themselves, and were convinced not by what they'd heard but by what they saw for themselves. Let me quote from Canon Douglas Webster:

> The communication of the Gospel is by seeing as well as hearing. This double strand runs through all the Bible: image and word; vision and voice; opening the eyes of the blind, unstopping the ears of the deaf. Jesus is the word of God. Jesus is the image of God. The word became visible, the image became audible. Now the verbal element in evangelism is clear. Where is the visual?

And the answer is: in Gospel churches, communities that are changed by the power of the Gospel.

So I end on that note. No church can spread the Gospel if it doesn't embody the Gospel. If a church is contradicting by its life what it is professing with its lips, then the credibility gap between what it says and what it is is so wide that it cannot be bridged by even the most energetic leap of faith. The church must seem like what it is talking about. It has to embody the Gospel of liberation. So may God enable us in our churches to receive the Gospel deeply, to sound it forth loud and clear, and to embody it in our common life of faith, love, hope, joy, peace, and all the rest.

2. Christian Ministry: How Pastors Serve Both Word and People (1 Thessalonians 2 and 3)

Radical questions are being asked today about the nature of the Christian ministry. People are asking, what does it mean to be (in Paul's phrase) a good minister of Jesus Christ? Is there a place for pastors at all? If so, what are their qualifications and responsibilities? These questions are not new, but I think that today they are more urgent than ever before.

In chapters 2 and 3, the apostle Paul supplies a wonderful model of Christian ministry in his own attitudes and behaviour. Although in some ways we shall be thinking here particularly of pastors, I hope we shall be applying this to all forms of oversight in the local church. It's quite true that Paul was an apostle and Silas and Timothy were missionaries, and not all aspects of their ministry are intended as a model for pastors. Yet I think the principles apply.

A word about the historical context. The enemies of the Gospel in Thessalonica were criticising Paul, accusing him of running away from Thessalonica. 'He's not sincere,' they were saying. 'He's in it for what he can get. And when the situation got too hot, he took to his heels. He doesn't care about the church in Thessalonica.' Now there were the criticisms, and it may be that some of the Thessalonian Christians had begun, under this smear campaign, to have doubts about the sincerity of the apostle Paul. So here Paul describes and defends his ministry against his critics, both during his visit (2:1–16) and subsequently (2:17–3:13).

Two preliminary points come out very clearly in the first two verses of chapter 2. Two characteristics emerge of Paul's ministry, and, I hope, of every form of Christian ministry. They are, firstly, *Paul's openness*. Already, he has told the Thessalonian church: you know what kind of people we were (1:5). And in the present passage he emphasises this even more strongly. He says his ministry in Thessalonica was public; he had had nothing to hide. Glance at 2:1, 9–11. 'You know . . . you remember . . . you are witness . . . you know.' Happy are those Christians who, like the apostle Paul, exercise their ministry in the open, before God and men; who are well known by the public for what they are, who have nothing to conceal, nothing of which to be ashamed, and can publicly appeal to God and human beings as their witnesses. God is our witness. You are our witness. It's all in the open. And I tell you, brethren, we need more fearless openness in our Christian ministry today.

And then see *Paul's sufferings (verse 2)*. Before reaching Thessalonica, he says, he's suffered insult and injury at Phillipi. He was imprisoned, beaten, his feet put in the stocks. And then in Thessalonica he met opposition and a riot broke out and so on. Yet none of these things deterred him. On the contrary: 'We had courage in our God, to declare to you the Gospel of God . . . ' It's true, isn't it: people are willing only to suffer for what they believe in. So Paul appeals to his openness and his sufferings as witnesses to his sincerity.

Four metaphors of ministry

After these two preliminary points about his ministry, Paul goes on to portray it by using four vivid metaphors for himself. He describes himself as follows.

1. *A Steward (verses 3, 4)*. Stewards are entrusted with precious treasure, to guard it, and the particular treasure with which Paul has been entrusted is the Gospel. In verse 1, he reminds the Thessalonians 'Our visit to you was not in vain'. It had purpose, it was to bring them the Gospel of God. And the developing of this picture, that he came not empty-handed but with the Gospel, is his use of the image of stewardship. His sense of trusteeship and responsibility to God for the treasure has been put in his care very strongly affects his ministry. Negatively, (verse 3): his appeal did not spring from error, he had no false motives, and he made it without guile. What a tremendous three-fold claim that is! His message was true, his motives pure, his methods above-board. He was entirely free of anything devious.

But positively (verse 4), he recognised, on the contrary, his solemn responsibility to God. See how this shines out of the statement. Again, you can't miss his God-centredness. God has *approved* him, and having approved him has entrusted the Gospel to him. The Greek verb means 'examine for genuineness – it's used of coins as well. Ordination candidates make much of their final examinations, the passing of which is the gateway to ordination. But Paul concentrates not on a human examination but a divine one that is never final. It is continuous. And at any time we may fail the examination, and be put on the shelf and be no longer usable to Almighty God.

God continues to test our hearts; so God was the person Paul was concerned to please. 'We speak, not to please men, but to please God . . . ' Do you get that? We are seeking to please God, who tests our hearts. No secret of Christian ministry is greater than this fundamental God-centredness. We Christian pastors are primarily responsible neither to the church nor to our superiors. We are ultimately responsible to God. It's God himself, no church or bishop, who examined and called and appointed us, who has given us our message, made us stewards of it, told us to guard it faithfully, who goes on examining us, and to whom we are responsible. Now in one sense this is very discomforting, because God's standards are very high. And in another sense it's marvellously liberating, to be responsible to God and not to men. Because God is a more merciful judge than any human being or ecclesiastical court. He is compassionate and kind. And to be responsible to him delivers us from the tyranny of human criticism and enables us to ride the fiercest storms of human opposition.

2. *A Nursing Mother (verses 5–8).* He comes to it in verse 7: 'We were gentle among you like a nurse.' The Greek word may, and I think probably does, mean a nursing mother. Once again Paul begins negatively; he's about to declare his great love for them as the motivating power of his ministry, but first he declares that he is entirely free of unworthy motives. Verse 5: ' . . . we never used either words of flattery, as you

31

know, or a cloak for greed, as God is witness, nor did
we seek glory from men.' Now there, you see, are two
of the major false motives in the ministry; material
gain, and prestige. The two commonest selfish motives,
and Paul claims that he's free of them both. They didn't
motivate him in his ministry. Instead (verse 7) ' . . . we
were gentle with you, like a nursing mother with her
own children.' Isn't it a beautiful truth that a man as
tough and masculine as Paul could use such a delicate
feminine metaphor to describe an aspect of his ministry?

And it was very appropriate. What are the characteristics of a mother with her babies? He mentions gentleness first. And it's all too easy for pastors, especially
when opposed, to assert authority, and to throw their
weight about. Not Paul. He was opposed, but he was
gentle. A servant of the Lord must not be quarrelsome
or autocratic (2 Timothy 2:24). But then not only was
he gentle like a mother, he was affectionate and sacri-
ficial. Look at verse 8: so far from the ministry being a
means of gain, he simply gave himself for and to the
people. There wasn't anything perfunctory about it. He
loved them: he longed to serve them like a mother. A
mother's whole life is determined by the needs of the
baby. The household revolves around it. That was how
Paul felt towards the new-born Christians in Thessalonica. And I venture to say that in the ministry and in
all pastoral work – I know it's true of myself and I guess
it's true of others – we need more gentleness, more self-
sacrificing love, towards the people we're called to serve.

3. *A Father (verses 9–12).* The reference to a father
comes in verse 11. It's striking to see Paul combining the
metaphors of mother and father. For the third time he
begins with a negative statement. He's very anxious
(verse 9) not to be a financial burden to them. So even

while preaching the Gospel to them he also made time to earn his own living. Presumably to pay his board and lodging with Jason (we happen to know the name of his landlord in Thessalonica). He worked at his tent making trade, presumably, and he did it night and day. I think he preached in the day and did his tentmaking work at night. And they remembered his labour and toil (verse 9) – both words indicate strong physical exertion. And moreover they and God were witnesses that in all points his behaviour was blameless.

If you look carefully, at the metaphor in verse 11 it seems clear that Paul is thinking of the educative responsibility of fathers. His fatherly ministry included personal example, exhortation and encouragement and witness (this is what the Greek means). All these were directed towards urging them to live a life worthy of God who was calling them into his kingdom and glory.

There is a father educating, teaching, bringing up his children to understand who they were and what they were going to be. I don't think there's any need to deduce from these two metaphors that Paul is laying down a stereotype of sexual roles. Scripture, as I understand it, discourages this, and it's striking as we've seen how Paul combines both roles in his own ministry. What is important is that Paul saw his ministry in parental terms. His responsibility was to love the people committed to his care as if they were his own children, to give himself to them, to serve, feed, educate them, gently but firmly, in the discipline and instruction of the Lord. What an ideal for the Christian pastor!

4. *A Herald (verses 13–16)*. The commonest New Testament word for the preacher is the herald, and the commonest word for preaching is 'to herald'. It's the verb Paul has just used in verse 9, ' . . . that we might

not burden any of you while we preached'. In other words, while we proclaimed it like a herald or town crier.

Here he concentrates his attention on the message which he taught the Thessalonians. And (verse 13) he thanks God constantly that when he brought them the word of God, they welcomed it. How? Not as the word of men, but ' . . . what it really is, the word of God which is at work in you believers.'

Now that's a beautiful verse. It's a really important word for our understanding of the authority of the Bible and especially of the New Testament. For here in verse 13 is Paul's unambiguous claim that the message of the apostles was and is the word of God. Though he did not begin his letter with an assertion of apostolic authority as he did in most of his letters, and though he had (verse 7) renounced his right as an apostle to financial support, he now reminds the Thessalonians that he has an apostle's teaching authority. His word was God's word, and they had recognised it as such.

We're all very accustomed to the claim of the Old Testament prophets, that they were bearers of the word of God. They claimed it constantly. But here you see in verse 13 is a comparable claim, by a New Testament apostle, that his teaching is equally the word of God. Paul doesn't rebuke the Thessalonians for regarding his message too highly. On the contrary he thanks God constantly that they recognised and received it for what it truly was. It is a clear indication of Paul's conscious apostolic authority. He knew he was an apostle, and he knew his word was God's word.

Then he adds, at the end of verse 13, that this work of God is 'at work in you believers'. God's word is not only true, it's powerful. It's efficacious in believers.

Notice the careful balance. The word of God has no magical properties. It is on the contrary ineffective, unless it is received by faith. Its effectiveness is in arousing faith and then transforming those who believe. So let's rejoice together that the word that is now enshrined in the New Testament, the word of the apostles, is the word of God; and it effectively works in those who believe it and receive it with faith.

Now we come to verse 14, and we see that that's exactly what happened in Thessalonica. In response to the word of God, they became imitators of the first Christian churches, the churches in Judea. They imitated them both in receiving the word and in suffering for it. The Thessalonian Christians were mostly Gentiles and had suffered from their own countrymen what the Judeans had suffered from theirs, the Jews. Paul gives an account in verses 15, 16 of contemporary Jewish opposition to the Gospel. They hindered the spread of the Gospel of salvation, and so they were hindering Gentiles from being saved. Paul sees this as the terrible thing it is. To stop others being saved, to stop other people hearing the Gospel is one of the most terrible things we can ever do, and as a result, he says, they are filling up the measure of their sins. 'God's wrath has come upon them at last.'

Now reading these verses, we need to be cautious. Paul himself was a very patriotic Jew. He gloried in his ancestry. He longed for the salvation of his people. He said later in his letter to the Romans that he would be willing to forfeit his own salvation if they could be saved. And he also taught in those chapters (Romans 9–11) that God had not cast off his people but that he intends later to include them. In other words, we have to balance verses 15 and 16 of this chapter with what Paul was to write in Romans 9–11. It's a good example of the importance of interpreting Scripture by Scripture. So there's no reason to suppose Paul changed his mind when he wrote Romans, or that there is anything here vengeful or incompatible with the spirit of Christ. Nor of course is there any justification for Anti-Semitism. Paul is simply stating bald facts, that the majority of his Jewish contemporaries were rejecting Christ, opposing the Gospel and hindering the salvation of the Gentiles. And this was an extremely serious thing, and God's judgement was going to fall upon them as Jesus himself had plainly foretold.

The pastor's responsibilities

Now we have got these four metaphors clear we can, as it were, narrow the theme down and consider the chief functions of Christian pastoral ministry. There are two primary responsibilities to God. The first is to the word of God, the second is to the people of God. The stewarding and heralding metaphors belong to our responsibility to the word of God; the mother-father metaphors, to our responsibility to the people of God. So let's enlarge on these responsibilities.

1. *Our responsibility to God's word.* In chapter 1, we saw the word of God spreading, coming to the church and being received by it and being sounded forth. Now in chapter 2 he goes further and defines the message. Three times (verses 2, 8, 9) he calls it the Gospel of God, and twice (verse 15) he calls it the word of God. In other words, it was Paul's unshakeable conviction that his message came from God. His Gospel (he calls it that in 1:5 is God's Gospel. Paul had not invented his mes-

sage. So we cannot disagree with Paul on the grounds that he was ventilating his own opinions. He wasn't. He was an apostle, a steward entrusted with the Gospel of God, a herald commissioned to proclaim it. Every truly Christian ministry begins here, with the conviction that we have been entrusted by God with a message to share with mankind. To share, not our doubts, but our faith. Not what Peter Berger calls 'rumours of God', but the Gospel of God, including its ethical implications. Yet it's this conviction that is so disastrously rare in the church today. It has become almost tedious to read of church leaders today denying the faith which they have solemnly undertaken in their ordination vows to guard and to teach. Prominent theologians contradict fundamentals of Christianity without any apparent sense of shame. A few years ago it was the fashion to deny the personality of the living God. Now it is the fashion to deny the Deity of Jesus of Nazareth, and patronisingly to describe him as perhaps the most wonderful man who has ever lived. There are clergy today who preach God's word with diffidence and their own word with confidence. And it is a disgrace to the church and a stumbling block to the world.

The very first qualification for any authentically Christian ministry is a firm conviction that God has spoken in Christ and in the biblical witness to Christ, that Scripture is God's word written down for the instruction of all subsequent ages, and that it works powerfully in those who believe it. Our task is to guard it, study it, expound it and apply it, to the people to whom we minister.

2. *Our responsibility to the people of God.* Christian ministers are ministers of the word and ministers of the church. And Paul, having expressed his deep love for

the Thessalonians by the parental metaphors, maybe quite unconsciously and unselfconsciously gives in the rest of the passage (2:17–3:13) a marvellous illustration of his parental love. Let me remind you of the historical situation: the serious criticism of Paul that was being expressed both for his hasty departure and failure to return, and for his supposed lack of concern. Paul makes a fourfold rebuttal of the accusations.

One, *he longed to visit them* (2:17–20). He flatly denies both major criticisms. He left them reluctantly. The Greek word means 'we were orphaned from you'. He'd never been separated from them in spirit. And he had tried repeatedly to return (verse 17). We don't know whether it was his preoccupation with the Corinthian ministry, illness, or other circumstances, but Satan used something to stop Paul from doing what he desired to do, which was to return to them. 'You are our glory and joy', he says. He longs to return.

Two, *he sent Timothy in his place* (3:1–15). Now this had been a real sacrifice on Paul's part. He needed Timothy's friendship, he wanted his support, yet he was willing to be left alone in Athens in order to send Timothy to Thessalonica. He could bear the loneliness better than the suspense of waiting for news from Thessalonica, and fearing that the church there had been overcome by persecution. I want us to try to feel this suspense of Paul in our hearts. It's to relieve it, and to encourage the Thessalonians, that he sends Timothy (verses 3, 4).

Three, *he had been overjoyed by Timothy's good news* (3:6–10). It seems to have been a recent event. Timothy had come back, found Paul had left Athens, rejoined him in Corinth, and Paul was simply overjoyed with the news that Timothy brought. The Greek phrase in verse 6 means: 'Timothy has come to us from you and *evangelised to us* your faith and love'. It's really about the only place in the New Testament where the verb is used in a secular sense, of good news other than the Gospel. 'Now we live' (verse 8) 'if you stand fast in the Lord.' What an amazing expression that is! So much is my life bound up with yours, says Paul, that my life is your life, and *I* live when *you* stand fast in the Lord. And then, in verses 9, 10 he says that he cannot adequately express his thanksgiving to God for them and the joy before God which they have brought him.

Four, *he was praying for them meanwhile* (3:11–13). In verse 10 he asserted that he prayed for them night and day that he might visit and see them. Now in verse 11, he actually does the praying He tells them what he's praying for, that 'God the Father and our Lord Jesus Christ' (note the bracketing again, more striking still in the Greek where the plural subject has a singular verb) 'direct our way to you.' A prayer that was answered in the affirmative, because during the third missionary journey, on his way back to Jerusalem, he did visit Macedonia again. And he prays that the Lord 'make you increase and abound in love to one another and to all men . . . ' and so on through to verse 13.

In all these things, these four things we've just been looking at, a true pastor's heart is laid bare before us. Paul just loved those Thessalonian Christians. They were only a few out of the thousands he must have got to know in his journeys. But he loved them and he longed to see them. Absence of news filled him with anxiety, good news filled him with joy. His heart went out to them. In a word, his life was bound up with their lives. 'Now we live if you stand firm in the Lord.' Now I ask myself: what are these expressions? What is this loving and this longing, this intolerable suspense, these fervent prayers? I think we can answer those questions. This is the language of parents, when they're thinking and talking about their kids, and when they're missing them dreadfully, when they're separated from them. So we see this parental side of Paul.

Here are two indispensable qualities of Christian pastoral ministry: faith in God's word, and a love for God's people. A commitment to the Gospel and a commitment to the church. A commitment to truth and a commitment to love. What we need to do is to pray for those who are training for the pastoral ministry of the church. We need to pray for those who are responsible for training the future pastors of the church. We need to pray for all pastors and those who share in the pastoral oversight of a congregation, that God will give pastors to his church who, like the apostle Paul, are both faithful, as stewards and heralds, and loving, as fathers and mothers. And who are prepared, in the words of 2:8 to share with those who serve, on the one hand, the Gospel of God, and on the other, their very selves, so great is their commitment to the Gospel and the people. God give us pastors like that in the church today.

3. Christian Standards: How To Please God More and More
(1 Thessalonians 4)

It seems to me that one of the great weaknesses of contemporary evangelical Christianity is our neglect of Christian ethics, that is to say, practical instruction in Christian moral standards. Christians have become known rather as those who preach the Gospel than as those who live it. We are not always conspicuous in the community as we should be, for strict honesty, simplicity of lifestyle, happy contentment and stable Christian homes. Now the main reason for this, I believe, is that our churches don't teach ethics as they should. We're too busy preaching the Gospel, we're scared of being branded legalists: 'Oh, we're not under the Law,' we say piously, as if that meant we're free to ignore it.

To this neglect of Christian ethics Paul presents a striking contrast. It's not only that all his letters contain detailed ethical instruction. It's also that he gave Christian moral instruction to very young converts. Look at 1 Thessalonians 4:1, 2, 6, 11. Four times in one passage he refers to moral instruction he gave them when he was with them.

We don't know how long he stayed in Thessalonica. Luke says that he argued three Sabbaths running in the synagogue with the Jews. He may have stayed a few weeks or months longer on the Gentile mission field, but not much longer. So within a few weeks of their conversion Paul taught them not only the essence of the good news, but also the essence of the good life. He taught them not only the necessity of faith in Jesus but also the necessity of good works, without which the authenticity of our faith in Jesus is inevitably called into question.

There is an urgent need today, especially in Europe as the culture diverges more and more from its Christian origins, to take seriously the example of Jesus and his apostles and give plain, practical, down-to-earth ethical instruction. We live in a permissive, relativistic, immoral situation today; it is urgent that we teach Christian morality, and it isn't any harder today than it was in corrupt, immoral Graeco-Roman society, in which Paul himself was teaching and writing. And we must teach with authority. We saw in our previous study that Paul claimed that his Gospel was the word of God (2:13). Now look at the first two verses of chapter 4. Paul is teaching that if moral instruction is given with the authority of the Lord Jesus, then moral teaching has as much authority as the Gospel. 'Therefore', he says in verse 8, 'whoever disregards this, disregards not man but God, who gives his Holy Spirit to you.'

As we look at chapter 4, we see distinct paragraphs, each clearly addressed to a different group in the Thessalonian church. The topics are sexual self-control (3–8), brotherly love (9–12), and bereavement (13–18). We don't know for sure why Paul chose these three subjects. It has been suggested that they refer to the three groups mentioned in chapter 5. 14: the idle, the fainthearted, and the weak. We'll go on to consider each of those groups in turn.

1. *The Weak (verses 3–8)*. Now Christians in general, and evangelical Christians in particular, have had a reputation (sometimes a deserved one) for being pre-occupied with sex; so that whenever they hear the word morality they think sexual morality is what's meant. In self-defence against that criticism, we biblical Christians want to remind one another that we try to be realists. Our sexuality, we know, is part of our created humanity, and we need to assert it as a good gift of God. But we also know that sex has become twisted and distorted by the Fall, and it is surely as a result of the Fall that this God-given instinct has become the most imperious of human urges. So it is destructive, when uncontrolled, of human dignity, human community, personality and maturity. Uncontrolled sexual passion is a very destructive thing.

Paul recognises sex as a good gift of God tarnished by the Fall. He teaches two fundamental principles here.

Firstly, *sex has a God-given context: marriage*. Look at verses 3, 4. Now there is some disagreement among translators and commentators on how verse 4 should be translated, and there are certainly some problems. But most commentators take the same reading as the Revised Standard Version: ' . . . that each one of you know how to *take a wife* for himself . . . ' That's the way I'm going to understand it.

So Scripture, being the realistic book it is, recognises

the strength of human sexual desires. It teaches that marriage was from the beginning, long before the Fall, God's gracious provision for his creatures. And Scripture insists that heterosexual marriage is the only context in which God intends sexual love to be experienced and enjoyed. Of course, 'enjoyed' is the right word, as you know if you've read the Song of Solomon. Outside marriage sexual experience is forbidden.

Now at this point I think I need in all integrity to add an appendix, for those of us who are single and have therefore been denied the only God-given context for sexual love. What about them?

Well, to begin with, we must accept this teaching of God, however hard it may seem, as God's good purpose for us and society. The only God-given context for sexual love is marriage. And we will not become a bundle of frustrations and inhibitions and neuroses if we gladly accept this standard; we will only become so if we rebel against it. We need to say to one another that it is perfectly possible for our sexual energy to be redirected both into affectionate relationships with many people and into loving service for others. There are a multitude of Christian single men and women who have been able to testify that alongside a natural human loneliness and sometimes acute pain, there can be immense and joyful fulfillment in the loving joyful service of God and our fellow human beings. You see, God has given sex this one and only context: marriage. That's the first thing Paul teaches, quite uninhibitedly.

The second point Paul makes is that *sex has a God-given style: honour.* Marriage is not legalised lust. The fact that it is the God-given context for sex doesn't mean that 'anything goes', within marriage. We've all heard about the sexual demands that are sometimes selfishly made by one married partner of the other, in terms of aggression, violence, or cruelty. And we need to consider what Paul teaches in verses 4–6. Note, 'Let each take for himself a wife in consecration and *honour*, not in the passion of lust like heathen who do not know God, and that no man transgress or wrong his brother in this matter, because the Lord is an avenger . . . ' Again, there are various interpretations of 'in this matter' – some have thought it referred to 'in business'. But I think the Revised Standard Version is right, that the kind of behaviour Paul is forbidding is the opposite of honour. It's any kind of selfish exploitation of the marriage partner. We all know there's a world of difference between love and lust, between the selfish desire to possess the other person and the unselfish desire to express love and respect. As the old *Book of Common Prayer* Marriage Service has it, 'With my body, I thee worship' (or, 'I thee honour').

Indeed at the end of verse 6 we read, 'The Lord is an avenger in all these things.' For the Lord sees even the intimacies of the bedroom. He hates every form of human exploitation, and that includes sexual exploitation. And though there may be no redress in law, there is at the bar of God.

And finally Paul says that God has called us to holiness, not for uncleanness; and to disregard that is not to disregard man but God who has given to us his Holy Spirit.

Well, there are sex ethics for the weak. The God-given context for sex is marriage, the God-given style for sex is honour. Oh, it's elementary instruction, no doubt; but it's plain, it's frank, it's authoritative, it's uninhibited, it's straight from the shoulder, it's just what new converts need.

What impresses me about the whole passage is that it's what the experts call 'theological ethics'. It's ethics arising out of our doctrine of God. Why do the heathen behave as they do (verse 5), with total lack of sexual self-control? Because they don't know God. But Christains behave differently. Why? Because we do know God, and we know that he's a holy God. It's fundamental to the passage.

In our previous reading we saw the God-centredness of Christian ministry. Now I want to draw out the God-centredness of Christian morality. Look at verses 1, 3, 6, 7 and 8. You see, in one short passage, Paul brings together the will of God, the judgement of God, the call of God, and the Spirit of God; and he makes these truths the basis of his appeal to please God more and more. Now, brethren, we know these truths. We're not ignorant of them. They are the foundation stones of Christian faith and life. The call, the will, the Spirit, the judgement of God. We know them all. And every one of them is related to holiness. Well then, this will show us how to live so as to please God. We've got to live in such a way that we remember his call is a holy calling, his will is our holiness, that the Holy Spirit is a holy spirit and that he judges unholiness. And when we get hold of these things, and when we think Christianly about these things – why then of course we shall want to please God more and more, in holiness.

2. *The Idle (verses 9–12).* It seems clear that there was a group in the Thessalonian church needing a very different kind of exhortation. In 5:18 they are called, in the Greek, ATAKTOI. In classical Greek this word was used for undisciplined soldiers. So the King James version translated it 'disorderly', and for centuries it's been supposed that there was in Thessalonica an undis-

ciplined or bolshy group. But recently it has been discovered that the word had acquired another meaning by the first century AD, in non-literary or common Greek. It was used for playing truant. So it appears that the group in Thessalonica were playing truant from work – that was how the word was used – hence they were not 'disorderly' as in the King James Version, but 'idle' as in the Revised Standard Version. Paul doesn't use the word in the present paragraph, but he does elsewhere in the Thessalonian epistles and it seems certain that this is what he means.

It's possible – commentators have suggested – that they had misunderstood Paul's teaching about Christ's second coming, and had given up their jobs, thinking it was imminent. So to them Paul's teaching is very plain. They are to aspire to live quietly, not to get excited, and to mind their own business and get on with their jobs as Paul charged them when he was with them. Then (verse 12) they'll command the respect of outsiders and enjoy economic independence. Now Paul frames his appeal in terms of PHILADELPHIA, or brotherly love, the special love that binds families together. He uses the word because we are brothers and sisters in Christ. It's natural that those who know God as their Father should love one another as brothers and sisters. He doesn't need to write to them about it, he says; they themselves (verse 9) have been 'taught by God to love one another', and indeed they do love all the brethren throughout Macedonia. It's interesting how these churches of Northern Greece seemed to know one another. They loved each other. Nevertheless, although they didn't need any instruction, he gave them some all the same. Verse 10: he exhorted them to love each other 'more and more', and in particular to express that love by working for their living and not depending on one another.

Now we need to be careful how we apply this today. I don't think we're free to apply this teaching about work in an insensitive way to everybody who is out of work and drawing unemployment benefit. Unemployment today is a complex social problem, a symptom of economic recession. What Paul is here attacking is not unemployment as such, when people can't find work, but idleness, when people don't want it. Paul says that we should want to work. It's an aspect of our love for one another that we don't become spongers.

3. *The Fainthearted (verses 13–18)*. We have the phrase in 5:14 'encourage the faint-hearted', and it's possible that Paul is using this word to describe the sorrowing bereaved.

Now bereavement is a very poignant human experience. Most of us have had the experience, and however firm our Christian faith may be, the loss of a close relative or friend causes a profound psychological and emotional shock. It needs a very painful and radical readjustment that sometimes takes months or years to overcome. It also raises anguished questions: 'What has happened to the loved one? Is he or she all right?' Such questions arise partly out of curiosity, partly out of concern for the lost person, partly because we perceive death as a threat to our own security, and so on. It's understandable. In addition to all that, the Thessalonians had some theological questions. Paul had taught that the Lord Jesus was coming back to claim his people and take them to himself. I don't believe he dogmatised about the timing of this, but it seems at all events that some of the Thessalonians were expecting Jesus to come very soon indeed – we've seen that some of them gave up their jobs. And then others were deeply distressed when their friends died. They had thought Jesus was coming back before anybody died. How would the dead fare when Jesus came for his own? Would they be at a disadvantage? Evidently they had raised these questions already with Paul, and in verse 13 Paul begins to answer them.

'Those who are asleep' is a beautiful phrase for Christian death. It probably refers to the body living in the grave as if sleeping. And Jesus himself used the metaphor to indicate that death is temporary – one wakes after sleep. We are not forbidden to grieve altogether. Don't misinterpret verse 13. Mourning is natural and necessary. If Jesus wept over the tomb of Lazarus, then most certainly we are at liberty to do the same. What is forbidden is grieving like those who have no hope. There's a difference between Christian and non-Christian grieving. The philosophers, the Stoics and the Epicureans denied existence after death. But we have a hope. It concerns the coming again of Jesus. This is referred to in the middle of verse 14, the PAROUSIA or coming again. It was the official term for the visit of a dignitary. So Paul may be hinting that the coming of Jesus will be the visit of the 'Emperor', the personal visit of the King of Kings. We know from Luke in Acts that in Thessalonica Paul proclaimed the kingship of Jesus, for his detractors said of him, 'He preaches another emperor, one Jesus.' And here Paul is saying, the King is coming again, and we must be ready for the King's coming.

But the Christian hope is not just the coming of the King. It is that when he comes his subjects will be with him. Look at verses 14, 16. He's going to bring the Christian dead, the redeemed dead, the angels as well.

And (verse 14) God is going to preserve total impartiality between the Christian dead and the Christian living – neither will have an advantage. God is going to bring with Jesus those who have died. What a glorious truth that is! And having stated it, Paul elaborates the Christian hope in four affirmations.

The Lord himself will descend from heaven (verse 16). That we call the return. The Lord is going to descend in glory.

The dead in Christ will rise first (verse 16). That's the resurrection. Having raised the Christian dead, God is going to bring them with Christ, as we saw in verse 14.

We who are left will be caught up (verse 17). That, we call the rapture, because we're going to be seized or snatched away to Christ; the Latin word RAPTUS means to seize, and that's what the Greek means.

And so we shall always be with the Lord (verse 17). I call that the reunion. We are going to be caught up in the clouds to meet the Lord with them and we shall be with him and with one another for ever. 'Therefore, comfort one another with these words' (verse 18).

What glorious doctrines these are. No doubt there is a great deal more in Scripture about these events, but let's rejoice in these things which are plain.

What I want to ask you to notice as we conclude is that Paul doesn't only help these three groups with doctrine. He helps them by reminding them of the two major means by which Christians are sustained in the Christian life and led into maturity and security in Jesus Christ. And I want to enlarge upon those two things as we close.

1. *We are to please God more and more.* We're not to think of this obligation primarily as law, but of love.

Our heavenly Father, who made us, redeemed us, adopted us into his family, put the Holy Spirit within us, loves us, and we love him. Of course we want to please him if we stand in that relationship with him. And the more we come to know him, the more we develop a certain spiritual sensitivity, so that in every moral dilemma it is a safe and practical principle to ask, 'Would it please my Father?'

2. *Comfort one another with these words.* We all get discouraged. We lose heart, we lose faith. Now in that, Paul says, comfort one another. 'Encourage one another', he says in 5:11, 'and build one another up.' Of course God comforts us secretly by the Holy Spirit within. He comforts us by the public pulpit ministry. But he intends his church to be a community of mutual comfort. If only the church were a caring community! Comfort one another, encourage one another, build one another up, hold on to one another. This one-another-ness of the Christian community is very important, for by pleasing God and encouraging one another, we shall grow into Christian maturity.

4. Christian Community: How To Care for Each Other in the Church Family (1 Thessalonians 5)

We are all concerned for the church of Jesus Christ. All of us are concerned for its renewal. And this naturally prompts the question, 'What does a renewed church look like?' What do we, God's people, look like when we're living by the word of God and filled by the Spirit of God? In this final chapter of 1 Thessalonians, Paul develops two beautiful pictures of Christian people which should profoundly affect how we behave. First (verses 1–11) we're children of light. And secondly (verses 12–28) we're brothers and sisters in the family of God.

We are children of the light (verses 1–11)

This paragraph, like the foregoing paragraph, relates to the second coming, but some readers I think are too ready to lump the two paragraphs together as though they concerned the same issues. It should help us to see that two quite distinct problems are being faced in these chapters, problems that have always fascinated human minds, and not least Christian minds. The first is the problem of bereavement, it concerns those who have died: what happens after death? Where are our loved ones? Are they all right, shall we see them again? The second is the problem of judgement, and concerns us as well: what will happen at the end of the world? Is there going to be a judgement? If so, can we prepare for it?

Now it's evident that the Thessalonian Christians were anxious on both counts. And I think you'll agree with me that these are modern apprehensions as well. And Paul, realistic pastor that he was, applied himself to both these fears. We saw in 4:13–18 that he has dealt with bereavement and the Christian dead. Now in 5:1–11 he deals with judgement and the Christian living; how we can be ready for Christ the Judge, when he comes?

Verses 1–3 state the problem. The Thessalonians were asking about time and season. Not, it seems, out of idle curiosity; they wanted to make preparation for the coming of Jesus. They knew that the day of the Lord would be a day of judgement, and they thought they could most easily prepare if they might know when he was coming. And Paul here indicates that the solution did not lie in discovering the date of the Lord's return. No, the day of the Lord will come like a burglar in the night (Jesus had used the same expression), like labour to a pregnant woman. Both pictures tell us that Christ's coming will be sudden, yet there is a significant difference between the two. The burglar's coming is unexpected; labour is expected. What Paul is emphasising is that there'll be no escape. Once pregnancy has begun, labour is not only expected, but, all being well, unavoidable. So putting these two pictures together we may say that Christ's coming to judge will be sudden and unexpected (like the thief) and sudden and unavoidable (like labour). In the first case, no warning; in the second, no escape. Now that's the problem. If we can't know the date, and he is going to come suddenly and unexpectedly and unavoidably, how can we get ready?

Well, Paul explains that there's no need for Christians to be alarmed at the prospect or be taken unawares. Why not? Well, we're getting to the heart now of the argument in verses 4, 5. I am so anxious that we will really grasp the apostolic argument here that I want to enlarge upon it.

The main reason that the burglar takes people by surprise is that he comes by night. It's dark; most people are asleep, or if awake they're probably out at a party and the chances are they might even be drunk. So (and see verse 7), darkness, sleep and drunkenness are three reasons why people are not ready for the burglar when he comes. Just so with the coming of Christ. Will he come in the darkness or will he come in the light? The answer is, both. He's going to come in the dark and the light. For unbelievers he's going to come in the dark, but (verse 4) 'As for you, brethren, you are not in the darkness . . . ' You are in the light.

Let me elaborate. The Bible divides human history into two ages. From the Old Testament perspective they are called the present age, which is evil, and the age to come, the age of the Messiah. They are sometimes presented in terms of night and day. It comes clearly, for example, in the Benedictus sung by John's father Zechariah: 'The day shall dawn upon us from on high . . . ' (Luke 1:67 ff.). Now the Bible also teaches that the new age dawned when Jesus Christ, the long awaited

Messiah, came. He is the dawn of the new era. At the same time, the old age has not yet come to an end. 1 John 1.8: '... the darkness is passing away and the true light is already shining.' This is the key thing. The two ages are now overlapping. Unbelievers belong to the old age, and they're in the darkness still. But those who belong to Jesus Christ are transferred into the new age and are children of the light. Already we have tasted the powers of the age to come. And when Christ comes again in glory, the overlap between the two ages will finish.

So then, here is the point. Whether we are ready for Christ's coming or not depends on which age we're in. To which age do you belong? Are you still in the darkness, or are you in the light?

Now verses 4–8 become quite clear, once we have grasped the biblical teaching about the two ages. The imagery of day and night is continued right through these verses. Notice it's a *day* that is coming. We are not children of the night. So don't let us sleep as the rest of the world does; let us keep awake and be sober. 'Since we belong to the day,' (that's a crucial phrase, the day that dawned when Christ came), 'let us be sober and put on the breastplate of faith and love, our armour, and for a helmet the hope of salvation.' Now I hope it's clear. If we are Christians and belong to Christ, we've entered the new age of light. Therefore let our behaviour be daytime behaviour. Let's not sleep, let's not live in our pyjamas. Let's stay awake, let's get up, be sober, alert, let's put on the armour of light, because we belong to the day. And then we shall be ready when the day of the Lord comes. It will be sudden and unexpected, but it won't take us by surprise, because we're ready.

The section ends, like the previous paragraph, with an exhortation to mutual encouragement. Glance on to verse 11, which is so similar to verse 18 of the previous chapter. As we saw in the previous study, the Christian church is a community of mutal comfort, edification and encouragement. It's with these words, this doctrine, that they are to comfort one another.

Now in saying this I have not forgotten one of the lessons of the book of Job and his so-called comforters. We have to give them credit that at first, for seven days and nights, they sat in silent sympathy where he sat. And one rather wishes they'd kept their mouths shut when the week ended. Instead they drowned him in a torrent of cold, traditional words, until in the last chapter God appears and contradicts the cold comfort these men gave. Their mistake, however, was not that they talked. It was that they talked nonsense. Generally speaking, words do encourage. Words do comfort. And we can derive great comfort from Christian doctrine as we stay our minds on these truths.

So what Paul gave the Thessalonians and urged them to give to one another in their anxieties about bereavement and judgement was not soothing, contentless words, but the foundation truths of the Christian Gospel. He says, I don't want you to be ignorant. I want you to know these truths, and stay your minds on them. What truths were they? The truth of the second coming of Christ is only part of the answer. That's what he refers to in these two paragraphs. But the major truth from which they were to derive comfort wasn't just that Jesus is coming again – that strikes some people with terror. It is rather that he who is coming again is the very same person who died and rose again. It is this truth that is at the heart of both sections. Glance back to 4:14. When Jesus comes he will bring with him those who've died. But the one who's coming is the one who died and rose again. Look at 5:9, 10. The one who is coming to complete our salvation is the one who died for us, that whether we wake or sleep we might live with him. So when he died he overcame the two great enemies of mankind, sin and death. And if we are united to Jesus Christ, neither sin nor death can ever separate us from him. Nothing can come between us. This is the emphasis. Read 4:14, and then 5:10. 'With him . . . With him.' Did you notice the repetition? The supreme achievement of the death and resurrection of Jesus is to bring us into a personal union with him. A union with him which nothing, neither death, nor bereavement, nor judgement, could ever destroy. 'Therefore comfort one another with these words.'

We are brothers and sisters in the family of God (verses 12–28)

The key word of this paragraph is: brethren. Brothers and sisters. It's the commonest word in the New Testament for Christians. It occurs seventeen times in this whole letter and five times in this paragraph, verses 12, 14, 25, 26, 27. The word bears witness to our common membership of the family of God. Our belonging to one another. We don't only belong to the day, but we belong to the family, and it profoundly affects our relationships with one another and our life and behaviour in the church. So what Paul does in these verses is to take up three aspects of the life of the local church, all items of contemporary debate and discussion, and give important instruction about each of them.

1. *The Pastorate (verses 12, 13)*. Historically speaking, the church of Jesus Christ has lurched unsteadily from one unbiblical extreme to the other in this area. Sometimes we have veered towards the extreme of *clericalism,* in which the clergy have dominated the scene, monopolised the leadership of the ministry, and received from the laity, the congregation, an exaggerated and quite improper deference; while the laity have been well and truly sat on, the only contribution desired from them being their presence on Sunday to fill otherwise empty pews, and of course their cash as well. That's clericalism; suppressing the people of God by clergy.

At other times we veer towards the opposite extreme of *anti-clericalism.* And nowadays we thank God that we are recovering the doctrine of the church as the body of Christ and the concept of an 'every-member' ministry. Every member of the body of Christ exercising his or her gift to the common good. But sometimes when recovering this glorious concept of the 'every-member' ministry, people go too far in that direction and say 'Well, the clergy are obviously redundant. We're all ministers now, so let's fire the lot, we can do better without them.' That too is an unbiblical extreme. There is a place at least for some sort of pastoral oversight in every congregation. Now I want you to observe how Paul, with this wonderful balance that the Holy Spirit has given him, will not allow either extreme in the church. So we notice how he describes the pastors and then how he describes what attitude of the congregation to them should be.

Describing pastors, he uses three expressions, with only one pronoun covering the three. Firstly, *those who labour among you.* A significant expression, because

58

some regard the pastorate as a sinecure. On the contrary, says Paul, they labour – the Greek word means hard work, it's the word Paul uses for his tentmaking – among you. The picture this word conjures up is one of rippling muscles and pouring sweat.

Secondly, *those who are over you in the Lord, your spiritual leaders.* The Greek verb is interesting. It means to preside, or direct and rule, and it is used of a variety of officials and superintendents and managers and chiefs and so on. But it also came to mean to protect, to care for, and to help. Consequently it was used for parents, who not only managed the home but also cared for the children. I suspect we need to combine in our understanding of this Greek word the concepts of managing and caring. We can't altogether eliminate the concept of authority from the verb, but we have to add that the form this authority takes (as we saw in chapters 2 and 3) is one of parental or pastoral care. And this is in keeping with the startling originality of Jesus, who taught that the first must be last, the leader the servant, and the master the slave.

Thirdly, *those who admonish you.* The pastor's teaching ministry includes the responsibility to warn, and even rebuke.

So these three expressions leave us in no doubt that Paul envisaged a distinct group of leaders in the congregation. What attitude was the congregation to adopt towards its leaders? Well, it was neither to despise them nor to fawn upon them, but to respect them (verse 12), to appreciate them and esteem them highly in love, because of their work. In other words, to have for them, because of their pastoral labours, an affectionate Christian regard.

Brethren, you know, don't you, that there are many

churches where the pastor and congregation are at loggerheads with one another. And it is a very sad situation. By contrast, happy is that church family in which clergy and laity, or pastors and people, live at peace with one another, recognising that God calls different people to different ministries. Happy is the church family in which the pastors exercise their authority not in autocracy but in loving care. Happy is the church family in which the congregation gives to its leaders the respect and love which their God-given work demands. And then they will live at peace with one another.

2. *The Fellowship (verse 14, 15).* Notice that although in verses 12, 13 some sort of pastorate is envisaged, in verses 14, 15 Paul addresses his exhortations to all church members to accept responsibility for one another. This seems to me very important. The existence of a pastorate is not to exempt us from this brotherly, sisterly responsibility for each other. He's addressing his exhortation to the whole congregation. He begins with the three categories we thought about in our previous study: the idle, the fainthearted (maybe the bereaved) and the weak (maybe the sexually uncontrolled). Admonish, encourage, support, and then be patient with them all, says Paul (verse 14). For they are in a way the problem children of the family of God. They have problems of doctrine, character, and conduct.

Of course we're all problem children in a way. And we're not to grow impatient with problem children because they're difficult and demanding. On the contrary we are to be long-suffering towards them. To me it is a very beautiful thing to see Paul's vision of the local church, not only as a community of mutual comfort but of mutual support; a genuine family.

From these particulars, Paul goes on to the general behaviour in the fellowship. Look at verse 15. All retaliation is forbidden to the followers of Jesus. Instead we're to be kind to everybody. Now what an extraordinary exhortation that is! An exhortation to the whole church. All of you see to it. Paul lays upon the congregation the responsibility for ensuring that all its members are following the teaching of Jesus. It's a responsibility that is not to be left to the pastors alone. It is not an exhortation to pastors but to all the brethren in the fellowship. A one-anotherness of mutual responsibility in the family of God.

3. *The Worship (verses 16–28)*. On first reading this you might not think it has much to do with public worship. But I want to suggest to you that it *is* a public situation that Paul has in mind. For one thing, all the verbs are plural. For another, the prophesying of verse 20 is obviously public. The holy kiss of verse 26 can't be given to yourself. And in verse 27, the public reading of the letter is required. So Paul has in mind public worship, when the people come together. Public worship is an extremely important part of the local congregation's life – some of us evangelical Christians are far too slovenly in our attitudes to it – and Paul issues four instructions that relate to it.

Firstly, *rejoice always* (verse 16). Now of course you could take that as a command to every Christian to rejoice. But you know the full New Testament exhortation as in Phillipians 4:4 is to rejoice in the Lord always, and the main time we rejoice in the Lord is when we sing his praises and come together to worship. It's reminiscent of many Old Testament commands, for example in the Psalms. So I'm suggesting this is not just a command to be happy. It's an invitation to worship, and to joyful worship at that. Some of our evangelical worship is positively lugubrious! But every worship service should be a celebration, a joyful rehearsal of what God has done for us through Jesus Christ. So let there be organs and trumpets and guitars and singing, and let's make a joyful noise! Rejoice in the Lord, Paul says, always.

Secondly, *pray constantly* (verse 17). To this he adds in verse 25, 'Brethren, pray for us.' So if praise is one indispensable part of worship, prayer is another. The time of intercession in the service needs, in my opinion, to be much more carefully prepared than it usually is, and sometimes led by lay people rather than the pastor. They can often intercede better because they see what goes on in the world better than the pastor, who tends to be cloistered.

Thirdly, *give thanks in all circumstances* (verse 18). So in public worship there's not only praise and prayer, there's thanksgiving. There's a place of what we in the Church of England call 'general thanksgiving' when we thank God for our creation and preservation and all the blessings of this life, and above all for his priceless love in redeeming the world through Jesus Christ. The Lord's Supper, too, is nothing if not a thanksgiving, and in one way it is the heart of our Christian worship and our Christian thanksgiving. But there is need also for more specific thanksgiving, for specific blessings of which each congregation is aware. We're to give thanks, not *for* all circumstances, but *in* all circumstances. We may not feel like praising and praying and thanking, but we shall do it whether we feel like it or not. Why? Because (at the end of verse 18) ' . . . this is the will of God in Christ Jesus for you.' These are three indispensable aspects of our public worship.

Fourthly, *we are to listen to the word of God* (verses 20–22). Verse 20: 'Do not despise prophesying.' There seem to have been many prophets in the New Testament church, and all of us know that Pentecostal and Charismatic Christians are claiming that God is again in these days giving prophets to his church. This is a controversial question, and I don't want to be drawn into controversy; all I can do is, I hope with humility, to share with you my own personal conviction on this matter on which I've tried to think and pray carefully.

It's of course very understandable that God should have sent prophets to the church before the New Testament was available. At that time the word of God came to the church through apostles and through prophets, who were the living and infallible teachers of the church. Today, all of us have to admit, whatever our viewpoint, the situation is entirely different. We have the written word of God. So certainly there can be no apostles comparable to Paul or Peter or John, and equally certainly no prophets comparable to the biblical prophets. Otherwise we should have to add their words to Scripture and the whole church would have to obey. No, in the primary sense in which these words are used in the New Testament, there are no more such. Paul calls them the 'foundation of the church' (Ephesians 2:20). The foundation is their teaching, and that is finished. That really isn't controversial.

The question is whether there are today some kinds of lesser gifts. Certainly God does give to some of his people a remarkable degree of insight, into Scripture, or the contemporary world, or into his will for particular people in particular situations. And perhaps it would be right to describe this insight as prophetic insight, or a prophetic gift.

Anyway, what Paul says is 'Don't despise prophesying.' We are never to treat with contempt any message that claims to come from God. Instead (verse 21) we are to listen and evaluate it by the clear light of Scripture, by the known character of the speaker and by the degree it will edify the church. And when you've evaluated it, 'hold fast to what is good' (verse 21) and 'abstain from every form of evil' (verse 22).

Now we come to verse 27, an exhortation, couched in extremely strong terms, that the letter be read publicly. It's a quite extraordinary instruction. Already the Old Testament Scriptures were read in the public assembly, a custom taken over from the Synagogue by the early Christian assemblies. But now the apostle says his letters are to be read in the public assembly as well! The clear implication is that he regarded the letter as on a par with the Old Testament Scriptures. Furthermore – have you ever noticed this? – he gives them no command to weigh or sift his teaching. There is no need to sift the wheat from the chaff, as in the case of those claiming to be prophets. No, they were to listen to everything the apostle wrote, and they were to believe and obey it all. So clearly Paul puts his authority as an apostle above that of the prophets. So today, even if there is some kind of subsidiary prophetic gift of insight, of far greater importance for the church is the teaching of the apostles, as it has been bequeathed to us in the New Testament, and the public reading and exposition of the Scriptures. It's that which edifies the church.

So in public worship there are always these two complementary elements on the one hand, there is praising and praying and giving thanks to the Lord; and on the other hand, there is listening to his word. Thus God speaks to his people through his word, and they respond to him with praise, prayer and thanksgiving. Throughout the service the pendulum swings rhythmically as God speaks and the people respond. Moreover, in both aspects of public worship, we are to recognise the sovereign freedom of the Holy Spirit.

'Don't quench the Spirit.' The command comes right in the middle of all the other commands. The word for quench is used for extinguishing either a light or a fire in the Greek, and the Holy Spirit is both. We are never to put him out. Let him shine into our minds. Let him warm and burn in our hearts. We must allow him his full freedom to speak and move in the congregation. Much of our Christian worship in these days, especially in the traditional denominations, is much too formal, liturgical, and stuffy. The Holy Spirit is bound hand and foot, and gagged as well. But there is place for freedom as well as fixity and spontaneity as well as liturgy. And in my own conviction, it is a combination of the two that is more enriching than anything else.

So the conclusion. Paul has given us at the end of his letter an idyllic picture of the local church, referring to the pastorate, the fellowship, and the worship. And he touches on church members' three relationships: to their pastors, respect and love; to each other, mutual care and support; and to God, listening to him and responding to him. To me, the key word of the whole section is 'brethren'. The pastorate is transformed if the pastoral oversight humble themselves and recognise the congregation as their brothers and sisters. The fellowship is transformed when we greet one another with a holy kiss, that is to say, when we recognise that we belong to one another. And the worship is transformed as well when we say '*Brethre*n pray for us', and 'let the

5

letter be read to all the *brethren.*'

Yet this living-out of brotherly love and family life in the local church is possible only by the word of God. So I ask you simply to notice, in verse 23, that he is called the God of peace, of harmony, who desires the wholeness of his people and his church – that *he* will 'sanctify you wholly, and that your whole spirit and soul and body be preserved blameless.' The God of peace and wholeness. In verse 24, the God of faithfulness; and in verse 28, the God of grace.

So if our local church is ever to be a truly Gospel church, receiving the Gospel, proclaiming it, embodying it; and if it is to be a true church family, whose members worship God and love one another, then only the peace, the faithfulness and the grace of God can make it so. And therefore it is into his loving hands that we commend ourselves, one another, and our churches.

THE WORKS OF CHRIST AND THE GREATER WORKS OF THE CHURCH

by the Rev. Dick Lucas

1. The Blind See (John 9)

Let me share with you the place where these Bible Readings started in my mind. They started at John 14:12; 'Truly, truly, I say unto you,' says Jesus, 'he who believes in me will also do the works that I do . . . ' – and now a very surprising sentence that has puzzled a great many people, including myself – 'and greater works than these will he do, because I go to the Father.'

It was after a splendid meeting, when a group of Christian businessmen met to discuss together the implication of these twelve verses, that I went away with a determination to look afresh at this verse in particular and to find out what indeed Jesus meant by these works. And I discovered straight away that the word 'works' in John's Gospel is one of the most important words in the New Testament. Just as important, if not more, as the word 'signs'. It refers to many of the things which Jesus did, not just the miracles, and I'm going to choose four of these during these readings. And I want you to understand from the beginning that these works of Christ are meant to reveal to us two things.

Firstly, they are meant to show us *what God had sent him into the world to do* – they are really the works of God. As Jesus' life is one of perfect obedience, it is therefore one of perfect revelation. The works of Jesus in John's Gospel, then, are the very works of God for this fallen world.

Secondly, they are also *the works that Jesus has sent us into the world to do.* Now I find this fascinating, because what we are going to hear is a job-specification for Christ's church in the world. We're going to hear exactly what we have to do, what the greater works are. Because Christ has gone to the Father, there are greater works for us to do. What are they? That's the question before us.

Some of these works are catalogued in Matthew 11: 2–6;

> Now when John heard in prison about the deeds of the Christ, he sent word by his disciples . . . Jesus answered them, 'Go and tell John what you hear and see: the blind receive their sight and the lame walk, lepers are cleansed and the deaf hear, and the dead are raised up, and the poor have good news preached to them. And blessed is he who takes no offence at me.'

We're going to take a look at four of those wonderful works of Christ, which were a testimony to John the Baptist and are a testimony for us.

Let's look first at John 9 and the blind receiving their sight. I might as well make a very ordinary human confession and say that we are starting with this one because I think it is the easiest of all to understand, in the sense of grasping how John teaches these things in his Gospel.

I'm going to divide the material into three parts. The

Miracle, verses 1–7; the *Man*, verses 8–38; and the *Meaning*, verses 39–41.

1. *The Miracle (verses 1–7).* First of all, the setting (verses 1, 2). A blind beggar by the wayside; a very common figure in those days. There are quite a number of 'Blind Beggar' public houses, if you look it up in your telephone directory, testifying that not so long ago he was a common figure in our society. Sometimes today you will see a blind man begging by a station. In the days of Jesus, of course, he was a very common figure indeed.

He was blind from birth. You will probably know that there are more miracles that Jesus did in healing the blind than of any other kind in the four Gospels. Obviously in the dry and dusty climate there were many eye diseases, and many of those who were cured had probably only been blind for a few years. But this man had never had the capacity to see. He'd been blind from birth, indeed a hopeless case, and I want to underline that because we shall notice it in all the great works of John; they are all hopeless cases. A very common figure, then.

And in verse 2, a very common belief. You remember those visitors to Job's side as he was tucked up there between the sheets, wondering why on earth he was there, arguing with God. His visitors had that tight little theology that the Old Testament people had, that God would reward the righteous and punish the wicked and that (since they had no real hope of life after death) it must happen now. So presumably if they saw a man who was punished then he must be an unrighteous man. And here they were asking the Sister for permission to visit in her ward a man who was known as one of the most upright people in society – and there he was sitting in bed covered in boils! So they got out their little

'personal worker's tract book', with its neat little the-
ologies at the end, and said 'Job, nice to see you, hope
you're getting on . . . Ah, Job? Ah, come on, Job; what
have you been getting up to? Some hidden thing in
your life, isn't there?'

Now if you're inclined to despise them, that little
theology lives down your street at home, doesn't it?
Because when something happens to one of our neighbours, they come to us knowing we are Christians, and
they say 'Please, why has this happened to me? Do *I*
deserve it?' How often we've heard that, all of us!

To this theology Jesus makes a definite negative.
There is no connection in this case between this man's
or his parents' sin, and his calamity. But we'll have
something more to say about that in our next study, to
balance the picture.

Verse 3 then leads us on to the significance of what
Jesus is going to do, because he puts his emphasis not
on the cause but on the purpose of it all. And the purpose is that a work of God might be manifest. Now you
see, we're so used to these stories, it's so easy to read
them, that we fail to grasp the drama. Indeed John's
telling of the story is so matter-of-fact that you can
almost read the story without realising what you are
watching. There seems to be a significance even in verse
1 – not *they* saw a man, but *he* saw. It's almost as if
John is saying that from the moment he saw him Jesus
recognised in this man a purpose of God. It wasn't sin
that led him to sit there begging, it was the purpose of
God. Notice the word 'manifest' (verse 3) – it means
'revealed and opened out'. God has given us these
stories to make manifest to us, so that we can't miss it,
what is the work we're meant to be doing.

So this is a very privileged, very significant man. At

this particular time, God had purposed for a mighty work to be done. It is the work of God (verse 3), but it is also the work of the church (verse 4). '*We*', not I, 'must work the works of him who sent me.' We – you and I – must do this work. Jesus there identifies himself with the disciples. 'Him who sent me' – a very favourite phrase in this Gospel; Jesus is always the one who is sent. 'While it is day', that is, while the opportunity is ours. And that is such a fleeting opportunity, is it not, for all of us? 'As long as I am in the world I am the light of the world.' You will know that this is a tremendous theme of the Gospel, right from the beginning. As we open our morning papers and as we look at the twentieth century, we are peculiarly a century of darkness, aren't we? How optimistic were the philosophers at the end of the nineteenth century. But I suppose that there has never been so much suffering in any century as in the twentieth century! It sometimes seems, doesn't it, as though darkness is going to cover the face of the earth. But we're told in the Gospels that the darkness will not overcome the light. And who bears the light? The Christians.

I have only been to Africa a few times, but I think I could say that one of the thrills of going there is to see the light of the world shining through so many of the indigenous churches. As you read of the appalling things going on in Africa today you sometimes wonder why there is not more blood shed than there is. Until you realise that the light is keeping back the darkness. None of the morning papers know this. But it's the light of the church in Africa which is the hope of Africa. And what could be said of Africa could be said of our own country, because the darkness seems to encroach upon us, doesn't it? How can we stop this darkness? Only through the light. The kids in East London, partly in order to feel important and to have a cause to live for, are joining the National Front. And as we hear of so many kids identifying with these things because it gives them a banner to fight under, of hate rather than love, we wonder what on earth can keep the darkness back. And here we're talking about Christ, the light of the world, given to us, so that the darkness will not overcome us.

And then the *action*. I repeat, the unadorned simplicity of the account can deceive us. But nothing, before or since, is to be compared with this miracle. Jesus doesn't look for or seek to encourage this man's faith. This is a creative miracle done by the will and purpose of God. If we confuse the works of God today, such as the answers he does sometimes graciously give us – the healing of the sick, for instance – with the Gospel miracles, we shall begin to confuse ourselves about the nature of Jesus Christ. And we need to be clear, especially today, about who Jesus is. God showed us that he is a unique man by doing, through him, unique things.

What did he do? Well, we don't really know why he did these things; he spat on the ground, made clay, and anointed the man's eyes with the clay. It may be that a symbolism is intended – man was made out of the dust of the earth. It may be that spittle was thought to be medically effective. I don't think we can be dogmatic. But I think we can be certain that the application of spittle to the eyes was expressly forbidden by Rabbinic law on the Sabbath. My own understanding of these verses is that Jesus was deliberately and provocatively breaking the Sabbath. But I wouldn't want to be dogmatic about it. Now verse 7. How simple it is, isn't it? ' "Go and wash" . . . so he went and washed and came back seeing.' Compare that with magazine articles, well-written accounts of the emotional and wonderful experiences of modern cures for blindness. We turn back to verse 7 with a little sense of disappointment. And yet it's so characteristic of John that none of the emotional details are there. What matters here is what was done, not what was felt; as so often in the Bible.

2. *The Man (verses 8–38).* What John gives here are five short conversations, so that we may understand what people were thinking and saying at that moment. Let me say to you that you are going to be introduced afresh to one of the most remarkable lesser characters in the Gospel story. And more important, you're going to be introduced to a second miracle: the enlightenment of a blind man who was blind spiritually.

The first conversation was with the neighbours. He went home, it was the natural place to go. Look at verses 8–12. What doesn't come out in our English version is that this is full of imperfect tenses. And Dr Leon Morris has suggested that this is to give the impression that they were all talking at once. They don't believe it's him: he replies, 'I am the man'. The immediate answer is, 'How were your eyes opened?' He tells them, simply and to the point. He doesn't waste a word. He is an excellent witness. And John tells us this scrap of conversation straight away, to establish the genuineness of what has happened. The best way for us to start to establish that something has happened to us spiritually is at home, isn't it? Among the people who know us best. And here we get the testimony of the neighbours. A mighty miracle has taken place.

The second conversation is with the Pharisees, and I'm afraid you won't want to overhear this one so much. It's in verses 13–17. Verse 13 describes a formal sum-

mons, probably. They brought him to the Pharisees.
The miracle was done on the Sabbath; this will make it
hard for the Pharisees to take. John sets up this explosive situation. And they interrogate the man. Again the
witness is simple. Then we get a division, between the
loyalists among the Pharisees and the realists. The loyalists say: 'This man is not from God because he doesn't
keep the Sabbath. Quite clear, do you see?' The realists
see a little further: 'How can a sinner do such signs?'
And so there was a division among them. Alas, as we
shall see, they go the wrong way. And frustrated by
their division, perhaps recognising what a remarkable
young man they are up against, they throw it back on
him: 'Well, what do you say?' The reply is significantly
higher than the one he gave before: 'Well, I think he's
a prophet.'

In the third conversation the blind man isn't conspicuous, and we find the Pharisees and the man's
parents in verses 18–23. We need hardly say much about
this unpleasant episode. The Pharisees had refused to
believe the evidence of their own eyes, but after this
interview the implication is that they can no longer
deny that this thing has happened. The parents have
an unequivocable testimony. 'We know that this is our
son and that he was born blind.' But they say, don't ask
any more, because we simply don't know. Why?

And now you see John is laying another explosive
charge in his writing. It said plainly in verse 22 that if
anyone should confess Christ he should be put out of
the Synagogue. And if you knew that by confessing
Christ you'd lose not only your religious privileges but
also your social privileges – that you'd lose your friends,
not be able to go into the local supermarket, your friends
would pass by on the other side of the road, you would

lose your credit card – you'd think twice, wouldn't you? And so also the parents. I'm not standing up for the parents. They took the easy way out. 'Ask him; he is of age, let him speak for himself.' And off they go. Not involved, that's the motto of 1978, isn't it, really? No responsibility, don't ask us.

We come back to the Pharisees, verses 24–34. Will you look at verse 34 carefully? It's really rather Marxist, isn't it? They require him to confess his error. No evidence has been brought against him, but he has got to make confession or take the consequences. So 'give God the praise'. What they're saying to him is: 'Don't make difficulties, confess your error, keep quiet and all will be well.' They get a very simple and good reply. On the question of the Lord being a sinner, he simply says: 'I do not know, I can't enter into a debate on that, but what I do know is that I was blind and now I can see.' Isn't that admirable? And for all young Christians, who are dealing with those better equipped theologically, it's better to stick to testimonies, to what you know, as here. So, 'How did he open your eyes?' What a remarkably bold reply: 'I've told you already, and you would not listen. Why do you want to hear it again? Do you want to become his disciples?'

Now, let's just use our imagination. He's a youngish man, his eyes have just been opened. He is seeing in front of him, for the first time, the people who have been leaders of religion since he was a child in the Synagogue Sabbath School. And it is beginning to dawn on him that these revered leaders are not open to truth at all. It's not sarcasm. It's the wondering statement of a man who is beginning to see the real situation. 'We know that God has spoken to Moses,' they say, 'but for this man we do not know where he comes from.' In essence the blind man's reply is this. 'I've been healed by this man Jesus Christ, and I ask you, my religious leaders, to give me an explanation as to how he has been able to do it, and you give me this brilliant explanation: he is a sinner. That's wonderful. That's outstanding. Is that all you can say?' 'If this man were from God he could do nothing' – that is now where his confession has got. He knows that this man is from God.

They replied to him in the way people have always replied when they have no answer. They cast him out. 'You were born in sin' – a particularly nasty thrust, isn't it? Well, they say in effect, it probably was true that you were born blind because of your sin. That's the kind of person you and your family are. And they cast him out: 'You seek to teach us . . . ' Yes, indeed, little did they know that this young man was teaching them, they who were supposed to teach others.

Now, I'm glad to tell you that in the fifth conversation we come to one of the most beautiful short conversations in the Bible (verses 35–37).

The man has been cast off by the leaders of the nation, but Jesus seeks him out. He takes him seriously. 'Do you believe in the Son of Man?' And do you see, here is the answer of a man whose heart is open: 'I would believe, if . . . ' Isn't it because we know that there are many people in heathen places who, if they only knew, would believe, that we send many people out to do missionary work? It's for this kind of man that we go, isn't it?

Jesus said to him, first, 'You have seen him' – that is, 'with your eyes; you've got a visual understanding of me as the Son of Man. And it is he who speaks to you now, to your mind, and I'm enlightening your mind and heart. I have given you physical sight so that you can see me, and now I am going into the depths of your personality with my teaching, so that you can understand'. Do you see the two sides? And then, 'Lord, I believe.' And he worshipped him. There is no doubt, there is no getting away from the fact, that the blind man worshipped Jesus as though he were God.

There are few mountain peaks greater than that, in this Gospel. Will you notice where he's come from? He started by calling him 'a man called Jesus' (verse 11). In verse 17, 'He is a prophet.' In verse 33 he could say definitely, 'This man must be from God.' And now he is able to take the position of a Christian and say 'I worship you, Lord'.

3. *The Meaning (verses 39–41).* These verses are very important, because they point us to our own responsibility. Now, in verse 39 Jesus tells us that he did not come to judge the world. We know that from John 3:16 onwards, yet there is a slight paradox here. Wherever Jesus comes and speaks, judgement inevitably follows in the sense of a crisis, a division. Don't forget that every time you preach the Gospel, not only do some come out of darkness into light, but some go deeper back into the darkness. The man who was blind was coming to see. But those who were, or claimed to be, seeing – the professional teachers – were becoming blind. By the end of the chapter a party line has been drawn, they've all decided to hold on to this line. And they're in darkness. I find that very terrifying.

Some of the Pharisees ask a natural question; are we blind, then? They receive a devastating answer. 'If you were truly blind, you would have no guilt . . . ' This is very like what Jesus says in 15:22. What he means here is that guilt is related to privilege. That is always so, in God's economy. God is a just God. 'But now that you say "We see" ' – because you have the responsibility of teachers in Israel and have in fact led the people away – 'your guilt remains'.

Who are the successors to these guilty men? Certainly amongst them are unbelieving theological teachers in our seminaries today. People who are to be shepherds of the flock, but are themselves blind. It is those men that Jesus calls guilty men. They do more harm to the church than anybody outside it. No atheist or unbeliever can do the harm that these men do. These are the men that he is talking about in John 9. And they're alive today.

What then is the greater work that we have to do? Now you see we are half way to an answer. But it's quite clear, isn't it, that the work of the church is *not* to go to the people who are blind and give them sight physically. If so I should have to withdraw my subscription to some of the work that BMMF have been doing, to say that this kind of medical work was not our job. No, that's absurd!

Now Jesus has gone back to the Father, this unique miracle remains a testimony of what the church has to do. The greater work is to preach the Gospel and open men's eyes. Since yesterday, 200 churches have been established in the world. All the new members of those churches have had their eyes opened recently. This is a far greater work than Jesus could ever do. And it's happening every twenty-four hours!

Let me give you two verses to underline this. Acts 26: 18, the Lord's commission to Paul. Now, what is his job? To open their eyes that they may turn from darkness into light. Isn't that remarkable? It means that every sermon, every talk, every Bible class, every word that we speak for Christ must be an 'eye-opener'. We should so work at our preaching and teaching that people go away saying, 'I'd never seen that before.'

For there is a logic in the Bible. We know that only God can open eyes, and yet he tells *us* to open eyes; that's the privilege of teaching. As we open men's eyes, God, by his Holy Spirit, is doing it also.

Lastly, Matthew 13:19. A verse that's become very precious to me in this last year because I have been concerned at the lack of understanding of the nature of conversion and the exalted place that people give to Satan – as if he could really stop God's work. But Satan has no power! – but there is a condition. 'When anyone hears the word of the Kingdom, and does not understand it, the evil one comes and snatches it away.' You see the corollary? If the word *has* got in, if the eyes *have* been opened, if a person understood that word, however small, the devil has no power to touch it.

Let's get very clear the importance of an intellectual understanding of the Gospel. Of course it is not merely academic, but God has given us minds. He has given us a marvellous book, he's commissioned many of us to go and open this book to others and to put it into men's minds and hearts, to open their eyes to it. And the moment that it is understood and people's eyes are opened, the devil is powerless, however he may try to snatch the truth away.

That's the power of the Gospel, the power of the Truth.

2. The Lame Walk (John 5)

We're now on John 5, our second reading: 'The lame walk'. And for the headings of this chapter: the *Miracle*, verses 1–9; the *Interrogation*, verses 10–18; and the *Interpretation*, verses 19–30. This is very plainly set out in John 5.

1. *The Miracle (verses 1–9)*. First, then, the miracle, Rather than going through it this time verse by verse, I'm going to select three things to say about it.

Firstly, it is quite evident that *this story*, as all the stories and miracles in John's Gospel, *is an eye witness account*. When I was at theological seminary thirty-five years ago it was fashionable to say that John's Gospel was not historical, that it was merely a spiritual meditation on great truths. That fashion has changed, I'm glad to say, to something more realistic. I would recommend to you the paper that C. S. Lewis read to the theological students at Westcott House, I think in 1959, which has been published in a paperback called *Fernseeds and Elephants*. In this talk C. S. Lewis spoke as a Professor of English Literature who had given his whole life to discerning between fact and fiction. And he gives there his testimony to his belief that as he reads these accounts of the Gospel, he is perfectly certain that he is face to face not with fiction but with fact.

Verses 1, 2 show quite plainly that John means to root this story in time and place, in history. The vivid details are quite beyond the pen of a fiction writer. However, I want to say something in general now about the witness of John, and look in our next study at the details. The word 'witness' is a great word in the Fourth Gospel, and by witness to Jesus, John means telling the story about the historical Jesus. I mention that because the word witness (and testimony, which means the same thing) is used by us slightly differently. We talk about somebody giving their witness or testimony when they stand up and say what Jesus has done for them. That's a perfectly proper 'witness'. But it's important, I think, to note the difference. The testimony of a Christian is to Jesus Christ and his power in life today; the testimony of John was to the coming of God in Christ into the world. The testimony of Christianity is not that God in Christ lives in my heart – gloriously true though that is, by the Holy Spirit and through faith – but the witness of the apostles is that God in Christ lives in this world. I commend that difference to you, because you will find that most of the modern evangelistic tracts omit the historical witness. They tend to start, 'Jesus is alive today. You have needs. Come to Jesus and you will find those needs met.' Now that is of course to cut out the whole historical basis of the faith. The apostles did not start with the fact that Christ is alive today, as though that were all to be said. They started with Christ, a historical figure, and what he did, in word

6

and deed. So these eye-witness accounts are essential. Today we are facing for the first time – I speak only of London, but I have a certain amount of experience outside London in student work – a generation of students who do not know the historical facts. But this is an eye-witness account about a certain man, in a certain place, at a certain time, and what happened to him.

Secondly, *it is a hopeless case*; he had been there and ill for thirty-eight years (verse 5). Well, what's thirty-eight years? It's 1940 from now, isn't it, going backwards. That means that this man was paralysed in 1940 and has been a hopeless cripple ever since. And any intelligent person could tell you what would have happened after thirty-eight years of lying helpless. Everything would have withered away! What is called for here, therefore, just as in our previous study, is a creative miracle, giving the man something he didn't possess. Making something out of nothing. Of course, it's even greater than that, isn't it? Because if a man were to regain in some wonderful way the possession of leg muscles, well, he'd have to learn to walk again, with sticks, and lessons like a child. Now this man gets up, he is creatively made a new person, and he walks straight off, carrying his bed. He doesn't have to learn to walk at all. This is, just as before, a unique work, quite unlike anything we can see today.

And thirdly, and you'll understand by now what I mean by the phrase, *it was a significant work*. Look at verse 17, where Jesus in answering the criticisms of his enemies says quite simply these majestic words; 'My father is working still, and I am working.' So here is our theme, the works of Christ. And, remember, the greater works we have to do. This is the very activity of God.

And we may be certain, I think, that this happening,

this man, was chosen from many. It's important, isn't it, when we read of a man like this being healed, to remember how many were not. Look at verse 3. Were there a few people at the pool? No, a multitude of invalids. A multitude. And most of them were not healed! How important to realise that. It's one of the unnoticed things in the Gospels. Do you remember, at the beginning of Mark, when Jesus was curing people all evening, then he went away in the night to prayer, and the disciples came to find him. 'Come back, everybody's waiting.' Well, because of course all that night the ambulances had been coming to that village, people had been walking over hills and dales to that village. The whole village was packed with invalids. And Jesus says to the disciples, 'I'm sorry. I'm not coming back.' Can you imagine that? Everybody waiting, and he goes off to another village, because, he says, 'I came to preach.' He did not come primarily to heal. And these miracles are selective miracles. He chooses this man, who apparently has no particular faith. He is the one who by his own sovereign will selects that this man should be healed as a sign and as a work for the whole church to understand.

A significant work. And of course the key point is in verse 6: 'Do you want to be healed?' What does it mean? Now I think I have to say that reading verses 1–9 only makes it impossible to understand what Jesus meant. Only the interpretation later in the chapter will indicate to us what Jesus meant by such an extraordinary question. Well, I must ask you to wait for the answer.

Finally, in this significant work will you please not miss verse 9. This belongs with my first paragraph, because it's setting the scene. That day was the Sabbath.

And so the whole explosive situation is before us. There's no possible excuse for doing this miracle on the Sabbath. Before, Jesus had justified his actions on the Sabbath by saying it was urgent. But there is nothing urgent about a man who had been lying there for thirty-eight years. It's provocative. It is Christ going out of his way to set the scene, to precipitate a clash, so that he and this man may be noticed and he can describe his authority for his actions.

So much for the miracle. Let me say again, it's told awfully simply, isn't it? Those words in verse 8: how simple, how unpretentious. Just imagine what Hollywood would make of them. The New Testament is strangely different, isn't it?

It's a mighty miracle. A unique, divine work.

2. *The Interrogation (verses 10–18)*. It's an ugly passage, but we must go through with it, for John is telling us that when Jesus does his work, there will always be hostility. Again, I'm not going to go through it verse by verse, but I want to introduce you to the three parties in the story: the man, the Jews, and the Lord.

First, *the man*. Well, he's a little disappointing, isn't he, compared with our character in our previous study. Did you not come to love the blind man, with his boldness, his clarity, his unashamed confession of Christ? Well, this man doesn't seem to have the same strength of character. I don't think we can blame him for going off and telling the Jews it was Jesus who healed him. He'd just met him again. But I think we can find a clue as to the essential meaning of this miracle in verse 14. Jesus says: 'Do you want to be healed?' He then heals him. And then, he finds him, because he knows that the man needs further instruction. What is the meaning of this? What is its spiritual meaning? And here it is: 'My friend, see, you are well. Sin no more, let nothing worse befall you.'

Solemn words, aren't they? Here Jesus does something very unusual in the Gospels. He ties together sin and suffering. In our previous study we saw that there is no *necessary* connection, but here he makes it clear that there is a connection. So it is a very solemn statement. And it is meant to show us, I'm sure, that in this man's case his crippled state was an outward sign of an inward sickness, a spiritual sickness. And when Jesus chose, in his own free will, to raise him from that wretched bed of sickness, it was a clear illustration of the power of Christ to restore our lost powers through forgiveness, to set our feet on the walk of the Christian way.

So, like all the healings in John's Gospel, this healing is a double one. This is the story of a man who was a cripple and was raised to newness of life, who was spiritually crippled by sin and was raised to newness of life. And the sign that the bitter consequences of sin and guilt had been removed was that he was freely walking around.

Now if you think I'm reading too much into this, please will you wait. Because you'll find that, in the explanation Jesus gives, this is in fact what he says.

Now *the Jews*. It is quite frankly rather horrifying to see how quickly the Jews took up a determined position against Christ their Messiah. It's one of the purposes of the Fourth Gospel to make this plain. The Creator comes into his world, and the world won't have him. The Messiah comes to his own people; they receive him not. Don't forget that the Christ we preach or speak about is a rejected Christ. He's always been rejected, always will be, and if we are faithful to him we will have to share something of that rejection. We don't look for trouble. We're not spiritual masochists. But we know if we're faithful to Jesus, we shall never be a really popular movement, even though we rejoice at the thousands coming to know him today. Sooner or later every Christian has to know this.

Look at verse 10. Just imagine that such a miracle had been worked this morning, and I saw the man and I said to him 'It's the Sabbath, it's not lawful for you to carry your pallet.' Surely, the only natural thing I could say would be, 'It's not believable that you're doing it!' But to say, 'It's not lawful,' it's almost incredible, isn't it? It shows a mind completely closed to what is really happening. This is why Jews persecuted Jesus, because he healed on the Sabbath (verse 16). And don't underestimate the strength of verse 18. By the way, this is John 5, not John 9. Right at the beginning of the Gospel, the Jews sought to kill him. We still remember with shock the determination of the Ugandan authorities to eliminate Archbishop Janani Luwum only a short time ago. It's almost unbelievable that anyone should want to eliminate such a shining man who has no power to harm anyone except his spiritual power. And the whole Western church learned afresh from that horrid event that the powers of darkness have never lost their determination to eliminate the living church. What a comfort it is to find it's nothing new. It's not something out of keeping. Here it is in verse 18. Where Christ is at work there will be bitter opposition. The powers of darkness will come out of their holes and seek to eliminate and destroy.

Now, *the Lord*, and that's much happier, for this is one of the loveliest insights into his clear authority.

Jesus had broken the Sabbath. I don't think we can get

round that. Not only that, he'd commanded somebody else to break the Sabbath, for it was a clear rule that you were not to pick up your bed on the Sabbath and walk with it. So Jesus does have something to answer for. How does he get out of the fact that he has apparently broken the Law? By the way he always gets out of this difficulty, by announcing that he is in fact the Law-giver. He gives here a clear claim for authority over the Sabbath – a claim recognised instinctively by the lame man in verse 11. When he is confronted by the Jews, he says what seems self-evident. 'If a man like that tells you to do something, you do it. He has authority.'

But the extraordinary answer that Jesus gives in verse 17 is what we must spend a moment or two on. Here is his explanation for his work on the Sabbath. Notice that his work and that of the Father are co-ordinate. 'My Father is working in the universe: I am working in the universe. We do it together.' Furthermore, he gives a brilliant re-interpretation of the Genesis story of the Sabbath; he reinterprets the Sabbath rest. It does not mean that the Father can ever cease to work. The universe would come to an end if he did. So Jesus claims the right to do what his Father is always doing, and that is to work as he chooses, on the Sabbath day.

Incidentally, there's a most interesting comment here on the Sabbath. We are to cease from human labour to take part in divine labour. The essence of the Sabbath is not inactivity. It is a change of activity. It's a great blessing to give us a day of freedom from the cares of business and everything else, so that we might give ourselves to the work of God.

So here is a most luminous interpretation and comment, on the Sabbath, upon God and his relationship to the world, and upon Jesus and his relationship to God.

Now it's an old rule in the interpretation of old documents to ask, 'How did the people of the time understand it?' Verse 18 is John's answer. As you know, the Fourth Gospel was written later than the other three. John has time to ruminate on these things. And now he says, well, when Jesus said these things, it was clearly understood at the time. And that was why the Jews sought to kill him. Not only because he broke the Sabbath, but also because he called God his own Father. These words could be misunderstood. People generally talk about God as their Father today. We have to be so careful about this language. We are sons and daughters by adoption, not by right. Jesus is son of the Father because he is truly Son of the Father, and therefore he takes his place by right as equal with God. And the Jews could not miss the meaning, the tremendous claim. If people say that Jesus never intended these things – and this is part of the weaponry of some of today's theological radicals – what are we to make of these stories? Who could have made them up? Who could have thought of verse 17? I ask you!

So, in the interrogation – an unhappy little episode, but an essential link in the story – we see the man, he's a picture, a visual aid; and we see the Jews opposing Jesus, and we see the Lord in all his majesty making, right at this turning point in his ministry, the tremendous claim that the whole universe, the whole church, and your life also is only sustained because he, Jesus, is working with the Father today.

3. *The Interpretation (verses 19–30).* Let me say that it is divided into two parts of six verses, most beautifully and artistically written. And both paragraphs say the same thing, though the first is speaking about the authority of Christ now, here and now in this world,

and the second about the same exercise of authority then, in the life of the world to come, or, rather, at the end of the age.

Now the balance and beauty of this paragraph is almost beyond belief. First, we look at Christ's work in the present, which is God's work. And I say in passing that you will notice we are bound to honour Jesus as we honour God, and it is impossible to honour God if we do not honour his Son. It's well worth having verse 19 ready learned when you meet other people and discuss the other religions of the world today. We Christians must stand firm here. It does require from us, doesn't it, a certain courage as well as a certain courtesy and carefulness to say this today. We do have to say, if we're going to be faithful, that you cannot honour God if you don't honour Jesus. You cannot. What is the reason? Are we to say we are the only people who are right? No. But we must say that he is the only one who has certain divine authority, an authority that is twofold.

His first authority is *to give life* (verse 21), to raise the dead and give life. And to Jesus alone in the whole of history God the Father has bestowed the right to give life to men. Secondly, the Father has bestowed upon this one person, Jesus of Nazareth, the authority *to judge men* verse 22).

Now these two things are quite outside the competence of any other person, however great. Because all other men die, how can they claim to give life? Buddha is dead, every other religious leader the world has seen is dead. Secondly, when all are sinners, how can any other man in history claim to forgive sins? There is only one man of whom it is said that he rose from the dead, only one man of whom it is said he did not sin.

It is to this unique person that God has given this two-fold authority.

Look at it again. He has the power to give life, because of course he's the conqueror of death. And he has the power to judge men. One can't take it in, can one? We try to judge people ourselves sometimes. Perhaps you're a parent. You come home, your wife has a terrible hour or two with the children, and there's blood, toil and tears all over the place. And you come in from the office and you do the heavy-handed male, you know, who knows everything. You send one to bed and one into the garden and one to wash the dishes. And about half an hour later a little voice is heard complaining 'It wasn't fair.' And your wife says, 'She's quite right. It wasn't fair. You didn't stop to listen. You didn't understand at all.' Oh yes, you see, you may think you know, but it's impossible even to be fair in small things, isn't it?

Now here is a man who claims to have the right to judge every reader of this book, everybody who ever lived in this world, and in a moment decide their destiny. This is the claim that is being made, in all honesty and integrity, by the apostles. It doesn't matter whether you date John AD 60, 90 or whatever. Thirty years doesn't make any difference to anybody making a claim like this. It is a ludicrous claim to believe. Unless it is true.

Notice also that these two activities always go together in the Bible. The judge condemns or acquits. So the gift of resurrection life in the New Testament is always a sign of acquittal. If there's only one sentence here that is important, it's this: the gift of life, resurrection life, Holy Spirit life, is always *the* sign and proof that I've been acquitted. When I come under the lordship of Christ, he acquits me of my sin and raises me to life. When he saw that man that morning, he saw a sinner. At that moment he decided according to his own will to acquit him of all his sins. So, visibly, to persuade us that this was so, he raised him to newness of life. It's a visual aid, of course, not the whole picture.

That this is what he means is shown by the summary in verse 24. If we hear Jesus's word, and if that word is only spoken at the behest of God, then if we're to believe Jesus we must believe God. And if we don't believe Jesus we don't believe God. So, 'If you hear my word and believe him who sent me' – then that moment, you have eternal life. Eternal life has come from the far distant future and been brought into your heart now. Judgement is over. Paul would call that justification by faith; this is the Johannine version (which is simply to say that Paul didn't get his doctrines from anybody but Jesus).

Right, now we look at the second paragraph, and this is so simple it hardly needs to be explained. He says the same thing with regard to the great day. It's anticipated, of course, as we shall see in our next study, in the Gospel, when Lazarus comes out of the tomb. A picture in anticipation. Verse 26: isn't that a beautiful sentence? You see, the one who is going to judge all men was a man himself. Therefore (as the author of the Epistle to the Hebrews says) he understands what it is to be a man. The judge will be perfectly fair. And then notice the opposing sentences which follow. The opposite of judgement is – what? Life. Exactly what he's been saying all the way through. If God removes my guilt, I can live. But not otherwise. This doesn't mean a salvation by works. None of us can divide our friends into the good and the evil. We're too much of a mixture. What happens to the questionable ones in the middle? No, he's talking in absolute terms. All men are evil in absolute terms, in the Bible. And it's only when they've come back to God through Jesus Christ that they can be called good.

Let's summarise what we've seen. I want to give you a cross-reference tonight; Acts 2:38. This teaching of John – of Christ, rather – is the teaching of the apostolic company on the day of Pentecost. For the blessing of 'no condemnation' is always realised and shown by the blessing of new life. Peter said, 'Repent and be baptised every one of you in the name of Jesus Christ for the forgiveness of your sins.' You're acquitted. You stand at the throne of the Judge, you hear the verdict on the last day, you see this great book – your name written across it – and then he speaks: 'You're acquitted.'

Go out and live in the light of that acquittal; that's what justification by faith means. And what is the mark of that forgiveness? 'You shall receive the gift of the Holy Spirit.' The proof and evidence in your life that you will not come into condemnation is the gift of the Holy Spirit.

Do you know his power in your life today? His presence, giving you the desire to flee from sin, giving you that thirst and hunger after Christ – all those evidences of the work of the Holy Spirit? They are glad evidences of the fact that Christ has authority both to forgive your sins and to give you life; for to him alone has been given, by the Father, the authority to do both those things.

3. The Dead Are Raised (John 11)

We're trying to digest that astounding verse John 14:12 in these studies. We started with the healing of the blind man, where we saw that the work of Christ was to bring sight both physically and spiritually; then he commissioned the church to the greater work of going into the world to enlighten men. And then we looked at the story of the lame man who walked, and we saw that it was not only a miracle of Christ bringing a cripple into newness of life, but also a sign of his power to raise men from condemnation to new life. I don't think I quite had time to explain the significance of that first question, 'Do you want to be healed?' You see, that was a question asking whether he *wanted* the new life. And of course, every day, the church in preaching the Gospel is doing a far greater work than Christ could ever do, reaching more men in hours than he could in months.

Now we come to John 11. It's going to be a little more difficult to see how we do a greater work than Christ in this matter, because of course this is one of the greatest miracles of all. And yet, if we understand this chapter aright, I think we will see how we do a greater work today even than Jesus did.

But first the skeleton of the chapter. Verses 1–16 form *the prologue*. Then *Two Conversations*, beautifully balanced, with Martha and with Mary, verses 17–37. Then *the miracle*, verses 38–44, and *the epilogue*, verses 45–57, though I'm not going to touch that.

1. The Prologue (verses 1–16). Let me firstly touch on a number of themes that are now familiar to us.

First, *a hopeless case*. Obviously far beyond the powers of anything we could do, and, more, he's corrupting in the grave. Verse 39 puts it very well; dear, practical Martha. Here then is a person very dead. So John is giving us in this greatest of all works of Christ a picture of a hopeless case.

Then I want you to notice *a bold prophecy*. It's never wise, is it, to prophesy; you'd have thought politicians and economists would have learned that by now. It's quite astonishing, isn't it, how we can't resist it. It's awfully difficult for anybody to look ahead. But Jesus seems to have no inhibitions about looking into the future. We get so used to it we hardly notice it. Look at verse 4; he's so calm, so bold. Calmly, definitely, dogmatically, right at the beginning, he says this illness is not unto death. Verse 11: 'I go to wake him up.' Just as easy as that. Some of you parents may find it hard to wake your children up. But it's not that hard, is it? A sponge will do the job if an alarm clock doesn't. And that's how Jesus sees waking people up from death. In verse 15, he sees not only the miracle ahead but the consequences of it – belief. And in verse 23 and in verse 40 we see this very bold prophecy. Just see how bold it was. Here was something clearly outside possibility, and Jesus clearly announces it and repeats it.

Incidentally, that's a very interesting point with regard to prophecy. One of the Old Testament tests of prophecy was to ask the prophet if what he prophesied came to pass. That test ought to be applied today, of course. In the case of the great prophets of the Old Testament and in the case of Jesus, what they said would happen, happened.

And then there is *a real danger*. We've seen danger from opposition before, and now it's become much starker. Look at verse 8, and Thomas's pessimism in verse 16. And look over to 12;11; even to be associated with Jesus and share his miracles was to put your life at risk. So John is ringing all the alarm bells. To stand for Jesus is to be in real danger.

But there's another side – you know, the Bible is the most balanced book in the world, and John is far too honest and realistic a historian to lump all the opposition together as 'the Jews'. Note verse 19. A number of Jews – we read of two in John 1:41 – did receive Jesus, and here John underlines very carefully, so that you should not miss it, 'Many of the Jews had come to Martha and Mary to console them concerning their brother.' Well that doesn't necessarily mean that they were believers. It means that they were sympathetic. Does the phrase recur in the chapter? Look at verse 45. It wasn't just sympathy. There was conviction. What courage that needed.

But look on to 12:10, 11. 'On account of him [Lazarus] many of the Jews were going away believing in Jesus.' Isn't that balance lovely? Through the whole length of John's Gospel, you will find a growing number of Jews who come out and take a stand so bravely with their fellow Jew, Christ the Messiah.

Now the question that arises in this prologue is, what is the *spiritual work* that Jesus does alongside the miracle? It doesn't appear that Jesus does a spiritual work with Lazarus. In fact when he is brought out of the tomb, Lazarus disappears from the story almost completely. He walks away. No, the spiritual work that Jesus does is with the two sisters. And it begins to dawn on us that Jesus is dealing, not with an individual, but with three people; Lazarus, Mary and Martha. And verse 1 sets the scene by giving us the three names. Three individuals living together make up – what? – a family. John is telling us that Jesus loved this family, and this family stands in John's understanding for the family of Christ in the world. John loves this kind of allegory. Look at Jesus's love for the family, which is underlined more than anything else in the prologue (verses 3, 5, 11, 35, 36). Yes, he loved this family. 'Don't miss the point!' says John. And in the epilogue John reveals to us the way the allegory is used. The prophecy of Caiaphas (verse 52); that is the great theme of the chapter. The purpose of the death of Christ is to gather together the children of God. And who are God's children? Well, of course, they're his family. And this little family living together is a symbol, a sign in miniature.

Now you must surely have noticed another theme, and that is *death*. It comes out in verses 11–14. And you noticed, I'm sure, that Jesus is giving here to the church one of its peculiar treasures, a new name for death. They are to call it 'falling asleep', because when you fall asleep at night the next thing you remember is that you wake up in the morning. And John goes out of his way to record that curious little conversation with the disciples, when as so often they get hold of the wrong end of the stick completely. Well, they say, if he's only fallen asleep . . . No, no, no, says Jesus, 'Lazarus is dead.'

If you have an etymological dictionary, look up all the words connected with death. Like 'cemetery' – do you know what it means, from the Greek? It's the word for 'dormitory'. And you'll find that the language of the world has been extraordinarily influenced by the great Christian concept.

Now there is a further point. There is that very strange verse in the prologue, verse 6. A splendid piece of illogicality. Verse 5: 'Jesus loved Martha, Mary and Lazarus, so when he heard that there was trouble there, he rushed to help them . . . ' Is that how your Bible goes? No, neither does mine.

You know, this is the kind of verse that John writes so that people are woken up. It's meant to wake you up, that's why it's told like that. 'He loved Martha, Mary and Lazarus, so when he heard that there was trouble and bereavement, he stayed longer than he normally would before he went to see them.' Now why?

John's Gospel was written when one of the great questions facing the early church was this: they had been taught that Jesus had won the victory over sin, law and death, that he had broken the bands of the grave, and that they were victorious over sin and death. They believed Jesus would come again and take them to himself, indeed many of them believed they would never know the painful business of corruption and death. And you will know, from a number of letters in the New Testament, that Paul had to write to reassure them about those who were dying; there was no snag about death, they also would be raised again.

But as the century went on Jesus delayed his coming. He foresaw this, we know, in one of his parables, about a nobleman going into a far country and returning after a long time. He foresaw it. He knew it would cause pain and grief and problems. Doesn't he love us? Why does he allow us to suffer? Now that's a big problem for the world, though it's only really a problem for the world because of Christians. It's only if you have a doctrine of a good God that suffering is a problem. The real problem of suffering is for the Christian church. How can a God who has revealed himself to us in Jesus Christ allow us to suffer?

I was at a conference in Australia when I heard about that terrible crash in Thailand, when, on a picnic, so many missionaries went to be with Christ. What a terrific loss. What a shock to lose in one stroke, all those magnificent Christian workers. You're bound to ask, why does God allow it? Why is he apparently allowing Satan to get the upper hand in so many situations?

So in the prologue, John is putting before us a great problem that the Christian church had to face and settle and solve. The problem of death. Death in the Christian camp. Death for those who are Christians, and ought surely to share in the victory of Christ.

Jesus is set before us here as someone who is the master of death, who gives death its proper name – sleep – and yet is master of death even though he delays his coming. That is the theme, and that is the prologue.

2. *The Two Conversations (verses 17–37).* And firstly *the conversation with Martha (verses 17–27).* The real character of Martha shines out of this conversation, and we see her as usual taking the lead, much more on top of things than Mary; more practical and yet, perhaps, a little less sensitive.

Notice all the practical details which aren't particularly important to the story, like the distance of Bethany from Jerusalem. And note that Martha's, 'Lord, if you had been here, my brother would not have died', is exactly what the early church was saying. If you had come back, Lord, our parents would not have died.

The details are always fascinating, but let's stick to the main revelation here. Let me give you a heading. This first conversation is *a revelation of power to Martha.*

In this conversation you can see where Martha's hopes lie. They lie first *in the remote future.* She believes that in the last day, people will rise from the dead. Sometimes doctrines like that don't have much comfort do they? Well, Martha says, I do believe it. But it all seems very far off. Second, they lie *in God.* If you pray, Lord, she now thinks, God will do something: you're such a great pray-er. Well, you say, in that case, if her hopes were in the future and in God, she was a fine believing woman. What's wrong with that? Isn't that what faith is? Yes, it is. And it's therefore all the more striking that Jesus almost brusquely sweeps these two things almost off the counter, in the most startling way, by his answer, 'I am the resurrection.' He uses the 'I am', to say, 'Don't look into the far future. What matters is what I am now.' Bear that in mind. Christianity has something to say to people about death now, not just in the future. And – in one of the most daring things that Jesus does, especially in the Gospel of John – he takes her eyes off God and says, in effect: 'You believe in God, believe also in me. I am not going to pray to God about this. I *am* the resurrection.'

Now you could not have a more blasphemous statement, unless Jesus is co-ordinate with God. He stretches language beyond its grammatical limits – it comes out quite clearly in the English – to show his unlimited power. All the 'I ams' of Scripture are very compelling, aren't they? You know them well. But what are we to make of this one? As Bishop Westcott says: 'Not "I promise resurrection and life", not "I procure", not "I bring", but "I am".' A very startling and wonderful statement. You'll notice that he refers not only to the spiritual life but to physical life. There will be a resurrection. That is eternal, spiritual life.

In that statement Jesus shows us that he possesses the power to give the church its two great defences against death. The fact and hope of the resurrection, and the fact and experience of the new birth.

Just to show you that the early church put its armour on, turn to 1 Peter 1:3; 'By his great mercy we have been born anew to a living hope through the resurrection of Jesus Christ from the dead.' Do you see, hope is a living hope; because of what is on either side of it. Christianity is a historical faith, the resurrection of Jesus Christ from the dead is history. But that's not enough. We have a living hope not only because of the resurrection of Jesus, but because we have been born again.

I was taken into a cemetery once in Southern France to see the gravestone of a young English boy who had died in the convalescent home. It was in English except for one line in French. It said: 'John Snooks (or whatever his name was), born 1880.' The third line said 'Died 1902', or something of that kind, and the second line said 'Né de nouveau, 1896'. Born again, 1896. And of course there was no fourth line. Such was the message to the French passers-by. Born anew, therefore with a living hope. With the history and the experience of Christianity as our shield, we can face death.

And this is the weapon, the revelation of power, that Jesus is giving to Martha, and through Martha, to the whole Christian church. We may well praise God that we've got that revelation today. But of course, the question that must be asked is that at the end of verse 26: 'Do you believe this?'

We haven't heard much about faith, have we, in these great works? But now we can't get round it. The condition stated twice already in verses 25 and 26 is 'he who believes in me.' I want to underline that. We really must not give a living hope to people who do not believe in Jesus.

How wrong it is, though tempting, to speak words of comfort about death, without also giving the Gospel. We must not give to the world the privileges that belong to the Christian. If the world wants them it must come into Christ. The tragedy in the Western world is that so many think they have the privileges that belong to Christ without ever having the responsibilities that belong to Christ. Please notice that there is no distinction between believing the great propositions that Christ taught, and believing in his person. Jesus said, 'If you believe in me, you will believe what I say. Don't be ashamed of me or my word.'

'Let's preach good news,' I heard a Christian leader say the other day, 'but let's not bother about doctrine.' I don't know how you preach good news without doctrine. And if the doctrine of the resurrection of the dead isn't one of the greatest of all, I don't know what is! It stretches Paul to his utmost in 1 Corinthians 15. If you think you can preach that in those tiny sermonettes you get in some churches – you can't. 'Mr Lucas, the buses leave soon after twelve – there's only about nine minutes in the pulpit.' How depressing it is, isn't it, when you've got all these things to tell them.

And let me also say, you can't know Jesus without knowing about him. Most of the preaching today is about knowing Jesus personally, in your heart; and that's marvellous, but you can't go on to know him in your heart deeply unless you know something about him. Otherwise you will find you are worshipping and preaching a different Christ.

To believe in him is also to believe what he says. Martha trusted him – 'Yes, Lord, I believe' – but it's much more than that; she makes a statement of faith that is the highest we have reached, theologically, if I may put it so, in John's Gospel so far. 'I believe that you are the Christ, the Son of God, he who is coming into the world.' Jesus had often sat at Martha's table, and she's often bustled in from the kitchen to give him his fried eggs or whatever it was. And yet at this moment her eyes are opened to see this: 'You are the Christ . . . ' Is there anything quite like that so far? Marvellous. A revelation of power for Martha.

The second conversation is *a revelation of sympathy for Mary* (verses 28–37). Now I want you to notice again the beautiful balance in the New Testament. Here John, with great artistry (but, of course, telling us exactly what happened) tells us in a very few words of a totally different revelation from the preceding. Mary comes to Jesus, she says the same words; but really her heart is too full. Mary is the one who is more emotional by nature. We're all different, by the way. I am thankful that God doesn't turn us all out stereotyped. And here are two sisters, from the same family but totally different. This one is the more sensitive, thoughtful, emotional one, and she hasn't anything to say. She just falls at his feet. She repeats the words but she doesn't really want an answer. She just wants to fall at his feet and get the comfort from him that she can.

Now what does Jesus do with her? You will notice that his revelation is quite different. When he sees her weeping and the Jews weeping, he weeps. The writer of the Fourth Gospel is careful to show us the perfect manhood of Jesus. He can never be mere man, can he? But here we're back to the mystery that he is real man. Just like any other person before the grave of someone he's loved, he burst into tears. I have been asked why he should do this when he knew what he was going to do a few minutes later, and that's a bit of a puzzle. I think there are two things to say. Firstly, there's no play-acting with Jesus; there is a mystery in his re-actions. He is not wholly like us, and I take it that his tears are genuine tears of human sympathy.

But there's something deeper. The word 'he groaned' almost means 'he was angry'. Why was he so deeply troubled? The reason, I think, is a very moving one. It's that Christ had come to this particular family knowing that he was going to bring back this particular man from the dead. But because of his person, Jesus could look into the future, and could see that there were going to be many, many thousands of Christians in a similar position; and he was not going to be there to do it. He saw, in other words, the bewilderment of the church in the first and succeeding generations. He saw that in God's mysterious providence the redemption of the body lies in the far distant future. Though inwardly I am saved, outwardly my body, like anyone else's, decays. And for the moment I have to walk and die by faith, because when I die and when you die, Christ is not there physically. We have to hold on by faith. There's no help being glib and over-pious about this. If you have visited the sick and dying at all, then you will know that the very ill – even the dearest Christians – often lose the consciousness of Christ's presence; and this worries them and their relatives.

What then is Jesus doing? As he is revealing himself to this family he reveals himself as conqueror of death.

But he reveals himself first as the one with the power to give life everlasting and also humanly as the one who sympathises and would stand alongside us in every sorrow.

The Miracle, (verses 38–44). Now let's read these few magnificent verses – the most wonderful miracle in the world.

This little paragraph tells us about the mighty voice of Jesus. He speaks to four people. First he speaks to *the bystanders,* and he tells them to take away the stone. Why? Well, it is a very practical command to the bystanders to do something that will enable Lazarus to physically return to this world and this life (it's a very different story from the resurrection of Jesus, where the stone was rolled away not to let Jesus out – that was quite unnecessary – but to let the disciples in). Then he speaks to *Martha*, who has protested that this is a very indecent thing to do, and he reminds her as he so often has to remind us, to believe what he has said. I'm thankful that we've got a very patient Lord. It's amazing how often he has to repeat things.

Then he speaks to *his Father*. And this prayer is said in public, out loud, for the sake of those who hear him, that they might realise he has been sent by God. This is always his concern. And I think we ought to pray the same kind of prayer, humbly, because there are so many religious leaders and teachers in the world today, and how is anybody to know which come from God and which not? We should pray for our spiritual leaders, and all ministers if they're preaching Christ should pray, that God will so own their ministry that the people will recognise that this is the truth. Otherwise how are the people to know whether the minister from the evangelical church or the zealous visitor from the Jehovah's Witnesses is the messenger from God?

And then the last voice. The voice of *the Son of God*, who speaks, and those in the tombs come forth. How weak our voices are in comparison with that! Like the father who calls to his children to get ready to go out; and after he calls for the thirteenth time a voice comes from the far reaches of the house, 'Coming'. And nothing happens. Are you expecting to hear a voice from that tomb saying 'Coming'? How ridiculous it is to compare the miracle with anything that man has ever seen. Here is a power that can stand beside a tomb, and call upon a dead man, who is corrupting, to come out. And he comes out! We couldn't evangelise, could we, if we didn't believe in the power of the word of Jesus.

So let's draw all these things together. I think this story is a particularly good illustration for us, to understand the greater works that the church is called upon to do. This work, is it not, is without doubt the greatest of all his work in this Gospel. And yet he calls upon us to do greater works. What can that mean? Does it mean we have got to bring people back from the dead? I have heard keen Christians say this. I remember a fine young army officer being killed when his truck turned over on him, and some Christians in that parish were praying that God would raise him from the dead that he might have a lifetime of service. Now, is that really what God wants us to do? I sympathise with their desire, but I could never pray that prayer. Why not? Because of course the very last thing in the world that those who have died in Christ want is to come back. There is a very old tradition in the church that Lazarus was sad from that day onwards. If Jesus is telling the church to call Lazaruses back from the grave, we are not doing them a good turn. And that's why it's so helpful to see that Jesus is not talking literally in that sense about greater works that we are to go and do what he did by Lazarus's graveside. This is an exception, that we might see his power.

What are we to do? We are to do, of course, what the two sisters were taught to do. And this is a much greater work. We are to go out into the world and preach the Gospel, and to show people how to deal with that enemy against which we have no defences outside of Christ. Everybody fears death, it has all men in bondage. But we alone, the Christian church, can go out in the name of Jesus Christ and do two things.

By the preaching of the Gospel we can give men a revelation of Christ's power, both in the experience of the new birth and in the proclamation of our hope when Christ comes again. And there's something very practical in this chapter; we also have the greater work of standing by the graveside. Where would the world be without the sympathy of Christians?

Now it seems to me that what Jesus is saying to us, the church, through John 11 is this. We're not only to claim Jesus as the resurrection, but we are to stand there beside people and give them a revelation, through our sympathy, of the love of God. They're to know the power of God through our preaching, and the love of God through our presence. That is a greater work. That work is going on at this moment all over the world. All over the world in Christian churches Christians are scurrying out to comfort the bereaved, to stand alongside them, in the name of Christ.

And that, you see, is the greater work that the church is called upon to do. To learn the lesson of revelation that Mary and Martha were given, to preach the power of Christ and to show the love of Christ in the face of death.

4. The Poor Have Good News Preached to Them (John 4.)

John 4 is our theme, and we're going to study verses 1–42 only; and I am proposing to give you an introduction to these verses today rather than to go through in every detail.

Verse 34 – here is our word, 'work' – 'Jesus said to them, "My food is to do the will of him who sent me, and to accomplish his work".' He said this to the disciples when they had been sent off to get picnic materials, and they found he didn't want to eat anything. Because he'd had that wonderful conversation with the Samaritan woman; she'd listened to him, and he'd already begun to reap a harvest, and he was deeply satisfied.

The phrase 'to accomplish the work' is used in John's Gospel in two senses. First, that of redeeming work, the atonement; but also, and running through the Gospel the sense of a work that has not been completed and indeed can only be completed by us. And the work that Jesus is doing here is the church's work as well; to reap a harvest among the nations.

Incidentally, it's this work that is the reason that there *are* greater works for us to do; because Jesus himself didn't preach to the nations, only to the lost sheep of the House of Israel. But in this story and one or two others, we see that the great missionary call of the Day of Pentecost is anticipated. Jesus, however, only began to touch that work, in situations like John 4. And he was thrilled by it.

I was told once that the Fourth Gospel records only twenty days in the life of Christ. A strange way, isn't it, to write a biography? But John has obviously chosen his stories with care, and very clearly he seems to love these accounts of Jesus taking time from the crowd to be with individuals like Nicodemus, in John 3. And here in chapter 4 we see the Saviour of the world giving all his attention to one – you would have said – unimportant person. In recent years this passage has become among Christians the pattern for personal evangelism, and so it is; any keen Christian wanting to tell other people about Christ will find in John 4 the best training school that he can find.

I don't however want to look at it quite like that this morning, but instead to study the passage's emphasis, which is on the word 'Samaritan'. It's not just that she is an unimportant woman. Jesus has been driven out of the places he would normally have preached, and he turns to others – in this case a member of the despised, half-breed race, the Samaritans. A hybrid people, having the Pentateuch but divorced from the main stream of life in Israel. You will remember, in Acts 1:8, that Samaria is one of the first stations on the missionary express journey of the church. The lovely thing about this chapter is that it shows Jesus beginning to anticipate Acts 1.

Let me give you the main structure of verses 1–42. Verses 1–6 form a *Prologue*. Then *the Conversation of Christ and the Woman,* verses 7–30, and of *Christ and the Disciples,* 31–38. And a brief *Epilogue,* verses 39–42. And so I won't get caught out by not getting to the epilogue today, I'm going to start with the prologue and the epilogue.

1. *The Prologue (verses 1–6),* 'Doors that are closing'. The key is the verb in verse 3: he 'left' Judea. The original Greek word conveys the meaning of leaving something to itself, to its own wishes; withdrawing whatever control was exercised before. The reason for this significant word is in verses 1, 2. John the Baptist had been a problem, but now here comes a bigger one! More success, more revival. Jesus's growing success leads to growing hostility. Each of these great works begins with John setting the scene, sadly, in just the same way. It's interesting that the pattern is repeated in the events of Acts as well. Paul, chased out of synagogue after synagogue in Asia Minor, is as it were forced to go to the Gentiles, and establish separate Gentile congregations.

Verse 4 – 'He had to pass through Samaria' – can be verified by looking at the map. It was geographically necessary. But those who see a divine compulsion in this verse are surely not wrong. Jesus does not take a step that is out of harmony with the Father. And we may be sure that God led him there. But I don't want to lose sight of the human element in the story – it's so human! – it's a long journey, it's hot, so he sits down and a woman comes, and, with that unconventionality of Jesus, he asks for a drink. John loves to show us the human Jesus. And out of this human situation comes a very remarkable experience as he discovers, under

God's leading, that this woman is open to something more than a request for a drink of water.

2. *The Epilogue (verses 39–42)*, 'Doors that are opening'. I hope you remember that striking point from chapter 11, where John comments that 'many of the Jews believed in him.' I think it's a beautiful balance, because chapter 11 is the final climax of the Jews' hostility to Jesus. I've said earlier that John is rather a sad book, because of the repeated 'not' – 'Received him not', and so on. But I've rediscovered this glorious note throughout John, the word 'many'. For example, 7:31 and 10:42. It's almost a signature tune in the Gospel. And how much more it means in chapter 4, when we read 'many *Samaritans* believed in him.' I hope you share the same outlook as the apostle John. It's easy to get depressed at closing doors. But I hope you also believe the other side; that many, many are believing. And what happened in Samaria was a sizeable spiritual movement. It's very appropriate that the confession of the Samaritans after that two day retreat with Jesus is, 'We know that you are the Saviour of the world.'

So that confession – we've not seen a higher one in this Gospel so far, it could hardly have been grander – indicates that Jesus's ministry to the Samaritan woman has been fulfilled. And an insight has been given to the early church that right from the beginning Jesus was always going to be the Saviour of the world, that his arms were going to spread out wide to include all the nations and every tribe; yes, many were going to believe.

Doors that are closing; doors that are opening. As far as I can see, these always go together. I'll always remember meeting a missionary who had spent all his life in China and was 'out', and, as a pale young curate, trying to say some words of commiseration; I received a firm, though gentle, spiritual ticking-off. I was made to see what I had never seen before, that God can be trusted to open other doors when he closes some.

3. *The Conversation of Christ and the Woman (verses 7–30).* In this conversation Jesus is beginning to reap the harvest, as we have seen. And here he gives the early church a definition of what it means to reap. It is *to bring men and women to a full knowledge of Jesus Christ.* You get here the same gradual unveiling of who Jesus is and what he came to do, as you do in John 9. In 4:9, all the woman can see before her eyes is a Jew. In verse 12, she starts to ask him some questions about his identity. In verse 19, when he probes into the innermost parts of her life, her eyes are further opened – 'Sir, I perceive that you are a prophet.' In verse 29: 'Can this be the Messiah?' And in verse 42: 'We know that this is indeed the Saviour of the world.' There's the climax. It's characteristic of God; men and women gradually coming to knowledge of Christ, and that's what it means to be a disciple. I don't mean an academic thing but a deep conviction – 'I know.' An extraordinary thing to say! Their eyes have been opened.

Here John is simply underlining what we read in all the Gospels. There are two reasons why people's eyes have to be opened: first, so that they might know who Jesus Christ is; and second, so that they might understand that he is to be crucified. These are the two truths that one's eyes must be opened to understand if one is to be a real Christian, and Satan does all he can to keep us from understanding. That's why we have to preach and teach Christ, and him crucified. That's the work of reaping.

But there's an even closer definition of what it means to reap, in the five stages of this conversation. All of these are included in reaping.

(i) *Making contact* (verses 7–9). How does he make contact? Not by plunging in, saying 'I've got something for you', but by asking her to do something for him. Sometimes, you know, Christians are very bad at making contact.

(ii) *Arousing interest* (verses 10–15). The people we meet are all apathetic; so Jesus starts off, 'If only you knew what I was talking about, and if only you knew who was talking to you.' An essential stage in reaping. 'If only you knew that we people in the tent at Keswick have got the best news in the world – you'd come to the tent and listen to it! But you don't know.' And he uses the language of everyday. There's nothing of jargon here.

(iii) *Reaching the conscience* (verses 16–19). Well, that was a very hard thrust, wasn't it? 'Go and call your husband. I don't think we ought to go on with the conversation until he's come.' She blushed, didn't she? Hadn't got one. No, we can't go on with reaping until we've reached the conscience. Otherwise the work will be still-born.

(iv) *Answering questions* (verses 20–24). A real, important question. He didn't sidestep it. And the way he answers this question is most masterly. He gives her the right answer – 'We Jews are right' – and doesn't shrink from giving her the right answer; but he lifts it up onto a higher plane altogether and says, 'But really, you know, what is happening now is that God is looking for new worshippers. And amongst them – he's looking for you . . . ' Answering questions is part of reaping, please note; we can't duck them.

(v) *Bringing to a decision* (verses 25–26). Yes, that's essential. She begins possibly to procrastinate. 'We'll wait for the Messiah and have a good talk with him, and he will tell us . . . ' No, no, the answer; 'I who speak to you am he.'

Well, I must leave these with you to study, especially Christian workers. They're all part of reaping. And please note that reaping is *not* just the final stage, bringing a decision.

One final point about this conversation. It's interesting, isn't it, that at that point she goes off. But she's not running away – we know that because she's left her water-pot. She's going to get her friend from the city. Missionary workers among students in many parts of the world are discovering an important lesson about them, and it's this: these young people are so closely identified with their families, in every way, culturally and so on, that it's bad, even wrong to bring a young person to faith in Christ outside of his family. And workers have for many years been bringing people to a certain point and then saying, 'May we come home and talk with your family, and tell them, with you, what you've been hearing?' And they do so, and the missionary answers the often hostile questions of the parents, and the effort is to bring the whole family, and often the whole community, into the kingdom of God. And this story, I think, is a most beautiful illustration of the fact that Christ wants the winning of one to lead to the winning of the whole community in which they live. The woman doesn't feel able to make the decision on her own, so she goes to fetch the rest of the community, and together they make the decision. That's reaping!

4. *The Conversation of Christ and the Disciples (verses 31–38).* I'm going to summarise this conversation under two headings. The disciples learn, and we learn,

these two things. First, *the church is to be constantly sustained by her commitment to the unfinished work.* This commitment gives us immense satisfaction. It isn't only feeding, taking in, that satisfies the soul. If I am always taking in, I shall get congested, stodgy; like congregations that are so well-taught, yet there seems to be no movement. Bible knowledge without life, without activity – isn't the charismatic movement, and many other movements with the church today, a protest against just this sort of thing? So it is by sharing the word with the hungry that I myself am satisfied. It's a shock to visit modern Turkey – one of the greatest countries on our map, an enormous country – and to know that there are only a handful of true Christians; and then to look at your map of the early world and see Colossae and Laodicea and Hierapolis and Thyatira – all disappeared. Why? There are many reasons, it's a complex matter, but one reason is that they did not 'give out'. Evangelism died.

'My meat' – I think I prefer the King James version here – 'is to do the will of him who sent me, and to bring to a finish his reaping work.'

Secondly, *the church is to be constantly recalled to her commitment to the unfinished work.* Because it so easily takes second place, and then it ends up by being nowhere. 'Lift up your eyes' – and if you look, you will see. Part of what a Christian ministry is about is teaching Christians to look. The early church situation needs to be understood here. In the church there were those keen Christians who had been Jews, who said 'We must first teach the people the Law, all the great things of Judaism, before we evangelise them to Christ.' It is probably this preparatory work that Jesus has in mind here when he refers to the 'sowing'. But

114

what the disciples are taught in these verses is that there are situations where the harvest is reaped without sowing. As Paul learned on his missionary journeys, he could go straight to the Gentiles, and straight to Christ. And that was an offence to many of the Jews who had been converted. It seemed too quick! The preparatory work had not been done.

And often there's a need, isn't there, for preparatory work of many different kinds before people can fully respond? And yet – Jesus is saying to the church, 'At *all times* there are doors in front of you, and if you will go through *now*, you will find that the harvest is ripe.'

You must here use your imagination to think of the village of our Lord's day. Think of an English mediaeval village. When the harvest was ripe, *everybody* came out. There wasn't a combine harvester. Everybody in the village was involved. And Christ is saying, 'There is a priority work in which you are all to be involved: evangelism.' There is a confusion, often, about this preparatory work. There's the *theological confusion*, for example, over evangelism and social action. I've seen fine young Christians working in inner-city areas who have said to me, 'I have brought these young people through the most troubled and difficult years of their teens, and though I cannot say that any of them have come to Christ, I am satisfied that I have done God's will.' It was a very honest young man that said that to me. And of course it is God's will that we should help people through the difficult and troubled times; – but we ought not to leave the other undone. If we love our neighbour with all our heart, we shall want to share Christ with him. We cannot wait until social action is done.

We have got to sort out this theological confusion,

for undoubtedly the Enemy is trying to stir up trouble here. And it is true that evangelism not backed up by social concern will be hypocrisy. But here we are told to go and reap, without waiting for the preliminaries.

Secondly there's a *spiritual confusion*. In very keen evangelistic circles there's been great confusion in the last five years – it has spoilt the evangelistic work in the city in the early years of the seventies, when young Christians could be found talking about 'Fellowship', 'How to get the church right', 'Looking within', wanting to get a perfect church to which the converts could be brought. That always leads ultimately to something arid, weak and spineless. We can't wait until the church is right. One of the best ways to *get* the church right is to go into the world – that soon knocks a few corners off us.

And lastly there's *cultural and sociological confusion*. Ought we to disturb the settled patterns of men? What about the immigrants, who are obviously going to enrich our communities in many ways culturally? Ought we to wait, are we not to evangelise? There's going to be a great pressure in the next fifteen or twenty years about this.

Well, I ask you to come back very often to John 4. Don't say, 'We can't evangelise until this, or this, or this is done.' Lift up your eyes. The fields are white to harvest. You will find this work the most rewarding work in the world, and you will gather fruit for eternal life. If you want a life with eternal significance, you must join Christ in the great work of the Christian church, and reap a harvest among the nations.

THE ADDRESSES

THE FAILURE BEHIND OUR FAILURES (Hebrews 5:11 - 6:10)

by Archdeacon Herbert W. Cragg

The passage to which I want to draw our attention contains a number of things which, the passage itself confesses, are hard to explain. But I think it is perfectly clear from this passage that much of our failure as individuals and much of the failure of the church is due not specifically to disobedience, or to sins we might name in some sort of catalogue of mistakes and blunders, but to a general stagnation and widespread immaturity. If there were to be a text for this address it would be 'Let us go on to perfection.' That is the Authorised Version. Of course the word perfection is not the perfection of sinlessness; that awaits the glory. The word in the Revised Standard Version is 'maturity'. That is the meaning of the word. So the call of God to all of us is to go on to maturity; and a failure to do so is a failure to go on to know God, and a failure to go on to know God ever increasingly is the failure behind all other failures. It is fertile ground in which sin grows unchecked and Christ is dishonoured by unworthy behaviour.

In 5:10, the writer has introduced the theme of our Lord's priestly ministry, after the order of Melchizedek. He finds it hard going; not because the theme is dark but because his hearers are dull. So he must leave his theme *pro tem*, coming back to it in chapter 7. First, though, he comes to the condition of his hearers.

I want to leave just two sentences with you. The first is this: *Immaturity is serious.* And the second: *Maturity is urgent.* The seriousness is demonstrated by reference to three characteristics of immaturity.

The first is in 5:11, where the writer says that his readers are dull of hearing. Now that could hardly be in the physical sense, nor do I think it refers to intellectual ability. God has a way of revealing himself to those who are not intellectually bright. I think this phrase means 'sluggish in mind' – slow to work out, in life, the implications of what they knew already. It was a failure in application. The writer is saying, 'How wonderfully you took every word once, and as the Holy Spirit worked it in, you and he together worked it out; but something has gone wrong. You were bright once. You have become dull.'

I wonder how this sluggishness arose. From familiarity? There are many of us who have long been familiar with holy things, And let us be very careful indeed. This is the case with scores of evangelical congregations up and down the land. They could almost tell you what the minister is going to say the moment he announces his text. But what are they doing about it? Familiarity – is that why you have become sluggish in spiritual things? I remember asking a question once at a children's meeting and a bright boy put up his hand when I asked them to tell me, 'What happens when I speak to you?' He said, 'Please Sir, it goes in one

ear and out the other.' I think I have a word to describe
that: dull of hearing.

I sometimes wonder whether failures in application
may not even be due to the splendour of our fellowship.
Is it just that you love the fellowship? It's so warm and
cosy, the coffee is hot and ready. But a failure in application is a failure to honour God as my Master, my
King.

The passage goes on to say, 'By this time you ought to
be teachers.' The one was a failure in application, and
this is surely a failure in availability. The church of
Jesus Christ across the world is suffering from a failure in availability. Crowds of people in every land who
need to be taught the first principles of the Gospel
suffer. The church is bereft of many who should be her
leaders and her servants, her ministers and her missionaries. Immaturity is serious. The world cries out for
those who can speak of Jesus; but those who ought to
be teachers still need to be taught.

And then in 5:13, a failure of appetite. You are still
on the milk-bottle, says the writer, and therefore you
are unskilled in the word of righteousness, and therefore you are a child. Of course the milk is divinely provided. God knows how to nourish all his children, but
he expects a move from dependence on milk to a desire
for meat.

Dull of hearing, needing to be taught, still on the
milk-bottle. These are the signs of immaturity in this
passage. Do we not recognise them in ourselves? A
little girl went off to bed and shortly there was a thump
on the floor. Her mother went up to find her daughter
lying on the floor, seeing stars. The little girl explained,
'I think I must have stayed too near the getting-in place.'
Is this what is wrong? Immaturity is serious.

But it's also dangerous. In 6:4–6, the danger of apostasy is brought before us. From this difficult and puzzling passage I draw two things for our solemn warning.

I want you to notice that those referred to seem to have made a beginning. They were once enlightened – a term which the Roman Christians in the second century used concerning baptism. They had tasted of the heavenly gift – a term which had been used of the Lord's Supper. They had become partakers of the Holy Spirit, tasted the word of God, shared in the blessing of the Gospel. And yet they had drawn back. Like Judas, who had lived and worked with Christ in the fellowship of the Twelve, they had renounced the faith, treating Christ as an impostor. Let us be clear, this is a wilful departure. It's not an accident but the departure which so easily follows a trifling with spiritual things. Scholars have debated as to whether such a thing could ever in fact happen. Well, one thing I'm perfectly sure of is that this solemn warning is in the passage for a purpose. One thing is certain. This warning stands in Scripture as a reinforcing of the seriousness of immaturity, and as such we dare not ignore it.

If immaturity is serious, maturity is urgent. And what are the marks of maturity? I name two: *solid food*, and *spiritual discernment*. In 5:14, solid food is described as meat. You do not need to be old in years to acquire an appetite for meat. 'Of course it needs preparation. It must be fresh and tender and palatable. If you are going to nurture your young people with solid food it will have to be the sort that makes the eater say, 'The only fault with this is that it's "more-ish".' I believe there are thousands of people in Britain tonight longing for a good meal in the word of God. Do you get solid food? Do you make it clear that that is what you are after? Far be it from me to say that this is in any sense to be laid at the door of the preacher. Most congregations get what they deserve – some do not. May God raise up for us in our day a teaching ministry that the people of God may grow thereby. For maturity is urgent. It's not a case of 'Hallelujah-all-the-time'. There is an easy, cheap attachment to the Gospel today which does it no good and insults the great Lord of the harvest field. God's people are nourished on solid food, not sweetmeats.

And solid food will lead you on to spiritual discernment. The faculties (5:14) will be trained to discern good and evil. That is to say that there will be a standard of righteousness for reference. There are countless issues in life which people spend all their time debating, when if they will only get down to the Word of God they will find that all they need is not debate but discernment. Was this not what Paul prayed for the Philippian Christians? 'It is my prayer for you that your love may abound more and more with knowledge and all discernment, so that you may approve what is excellent and may be pure and blameless to the day of Christ.'

I wonder if you are paddling round in the shallow waters of an elementary faith, or whether you have begun to get down to the truths of the Gospel as Scripture enshrines and unfolds them. How? I just give you three suggestions from the passage.

First, verse 7: *drinking in the rain*. How many showers of blessing have fallen from the pulpit you look at every Sunday, that you have not drunk in? On the only occasion I have been to the Japanese Keswick, one of the delightful things was to see the people sitting on the floor and writing, writing, writing. They wanted to preserve what they were learning.

And then, *working out the salvation*. I find as I travel all around the land that there are folks in desperate need of somebody who will work out their salvation in relationship to them; the shut-in, the lonely, the hard pressed of every kind and every age. There's an abundant field for the out-working of the in-working grace of God. What you do not use you will lose.

Then, towards the end, *pressing on through faith and patience, to inherit the promises*. Maturity is not a second blessing; it's not a sudden blessing. It is a steady, ongoing blessing. You have got to work at it.

Immaturity is serious; maturity is urgent. Therefore diligence is necessary.

BE FILLED WITH THE SPIRIT
(Ephesians 5:18)

by the Rev. Ronald Dunn

They tell me it's rude and impolite to ask personal questions. You don't go up to a fellow to ask how much money he makes in a year. It's not really polite to ask somebody, 'How much did you pay for those shoes you're wearing?' I want to be rude and impolite for just a moment and ask you a very personal question: 'Is the Holy Spirit filling you right now?'

Understand the question; 'I'm not asking, 'Do you believe in the filling of the Holy Spirit?' I'm not asking, 'Have you been filled with the Spirit?' The question is, 'Is the Holy Spirit filling you right now?' There are three possible answers: 'Yes', 'No', 'I don't know what you mean – I don't know.' I want to present what the Bible has to say about being filled with the Spirit, and I trust the Lord will enable me to present it so that at least at the end all of us will be able to answer clearly 'Yes' or 'No'.

'Be filled with the Spirit.' Now I recognise that there is a good deal of controversy across the world today concerning the filling of the Holy Spirit, but neverthe-

less, simply because some people carry it to extremes and excesses, I'm not going to let them rob me of what is truly mine in the Lord Jesus Christ. I cannot read the New Testament without being convinced that we are to experience what the Bible calls the fullness of the Holy Spirit. It's a biblical precept, a biblical truth.

I used to have an illustration I used for the fullness of the Holy Spirit. I had a glass with about an inch of water in it, and I used to say 'The glass represents the Christian, and the water, the Holy Spirit – every Christian has the Holy Spirit, but he's not *filled* with the Holy Spirit.' Then I would fill the glass up to overflowing . . . Only one thing wrong with that illustration. It was *wrong.* It wasn't scriptural, for what I was saying is that the fullness means receiving more of the Spirit than I had before; and that is absolutely incorrect.

Now I know that there are those who say that we receive Jesus first by an act of faith and then later on the road, as it were, we receive the Spirit by a similar act of faith. I disagree with that. That would dissect the Trinity. It would destroy the harmony of the body of Christ. The Bible tells us we all *have* received the Holy Spirit and are indwelt by him. He is God's birthday gift to you. When you were saved, at that moment the Holy Spirit took up residence in your body.

No, I don't believe the fullness of the Spirit means getting more out of the Spirit than we ever had before. I believe it's the Spirit getting more of us – so taking control of our lives that he touches every area, every facet of our lives.

I used to be put off by two mistakes I made in this matter. One, I thought that being filled with the Spirit was only for preachers. But I discovered that it is God's standard for every believer. Ephesians 5:18 uses a plural; he says '*to all of you*'. On the day of Pentecost, they were *all* filled with the Spirit. The mistake I made was that I thought that the fullness of the Holy Spirit was for service only. I do not now believe that that is the primary reason we should be filled. I believe the fullness is primarily for *Christ-like living*. Look at the context; read on, and you'll find he talks about sharing it with another, about relationships, about husbands loving their wives as Christ loved the church, and so on. It is my conviction that the filling of the Holy Spirit, while necessary for service, is primarily for living a Christ-filled life in every relationship we have. I do not believe that I *can* love my wife as Christ loved the church, without the empowering of the Holy Spirit. I do not believe that I *can* rear my children in the nurture and admonition of the Lord without the fullness of the Holy Spirit. I require power, to live in the home as the right kind of husband that I ought to be – far more power than I need to preach a sermon. And I want to tell you something – I make a confession – it does very little good for you to preach a powerful sermon if, when you step out of the pulpit, you cannot control your temper. One of the great problems today is there is a great deal of saintlessness inside the pulpit and a great deal of sourness outside it.

No, if the home is to be as it ought to be, we need the fullness of the Holy Spirit. I've had couples coming to me saying, 'We've got a personality conflict.' I've found that a personality conflict within a marriage is nothing more than *my* selfishness getting in the way of *your* selfishness. If we are to eliminate that kind of selfishness it takes the power of the Holy Spirit to keep *my self* in the place of crucifixion.

The other mistake I used to make was that I thought

127

the fullness of the Holy Spirit was a reward that God gave us when we got to a certain spiritual plateau. I believed that we grew *towards* the fullness. But I'm convinced today that that is wrong. We grow *from* the fullness of the Holy Spirit. Now you can grow in religious activity and church knowledge without the fullness of the Spirit, but I very seriously doubt whether you can grow in Christ-likeness until the Spirit of God is filling and controlling your life. This is when the Spirit is able to fulfil his ministry in us and conform us to the image of Jesus Christ.

There are three things I want to share with you concerning the fullness of the Spirit.

1. *To be filled with the Spirit is a command of God.* A command. That's obvious, you say. Well, yes and no. We recognise it as a command. He's not making a polite suggestion, he's giving a command. And yet I think the average Christian never considers that a command. I believe most of us think it's an optional extra, a luxury item. Notice moreover that in verse 18 there are two commands, a positive and a negative, 'and do not get drunk with wine'. Now we all believe that and obey it. Can you imagine how you would react if next Sunday your pastor stumbled into the pulpit, drunk with wine? When we see a drunk we say, 'The Bible says not to be drunk with wine.' And yet that same verse also tells us to be filled with the Spirit.

Now if I understand the Bible at all, it means this; it is just as sinful for a Christian not to be filled with Spirit as it is for him to be drunk with wine. The problem is, we've accentuated the negative and eliminated the positive in that verse. We ask prospective ordinands, 'Do you drink?' We check them out on that, but we never ask, 'Are you filled with the Spirit?' The qualifications of those original men in Acts 6? – 'Look out among you, find seven men who are full of the Holy Ghost.'

As a matter of fact, I've had less trouble, as a pastor, with men drunk with wine than with men not filled with the Spirit. I've never had a church business meeting disrupted by a man drunk. I've had several of them disrupted by men who were not filled with the Spirit. I believe more harm has been done to the church by our failure to be filled with the Spirit than by those who are filled with wine.

It's a command, it's not optional, and we must understand that as we enjoy Bible exposition, yet we must make a decision. All truth is like petrol in a tank. It won't get you anywhere unless it is ignited. I believe that that point of ignition of the power of all truth is right here, at this point.

2. *The fullness of the Spirit is a command to be controlled.* There are many folk around today talking about the filling of the Spirit, but what they're really interested in is the *feeling* of the Spirit. They're after the thrill of the fill. The 'happiness boys'. They are always going around saying, 'If you'll just get a dose of the fullness of the Spirit, you'll always be healthy. You'll always be wealthy. Everything will be just wonderful.' I don't believe that Scripture teaches that at all. To be filled with the Spirit is to be controlled by the Spirit. You say, 'I want to be filled with the Spirit.' Oh, do you? Do you want to be controlled by someone who is so holy that he will not ever allow you to think of yourself first, will not tolerate your evil thoughts and desires, will want to possess and command you completely? And if you want to walk in the Spirit you can't push yourself forward.

9   129

In our church once I had the bright idea of re-organising our missionary offerings. The first year we did it the new way we tripled our mission offerings. Well, I want you to know, I was proud of that. I was proud it was my idea. Well, we were having a deacons' meeting and the Chairman of the Finance Committee was there, and he read the report and told about the offering, in glowing terms, and then he said, 'We certainly want to let the Women's Missionary Union know how thankful we are to them for coming up with this idea.' The minute I heard that, I was out of my seat with my hand up. And then I was reminded, 'Others may take credit for what they've done, but you may not.' I said, 'Lord, try me out some other time — Lord, anybody but the Women's Missionary Union — they get credit for everything!' But the Lord kept on, 'Others may but you may not', and I sat down.

You see most of the time when we talk about the full-ness of the Spirit we talk about dethroning self, and we usually mean the 'bad' self. The self that curses and steals and lies and lusts — but I have an idea that there is a 'good self' that is more difficult to give up. We are immediately willing to let the Lord take away the bad self, but Lord, not my Christian service. I remember the Lord came to me once and said, 'Son, I know you're willing to be used' — a man who is in the ministry would be a fool if he weren't willing to be used, and if God were to promise to make us all Billy Grahams or some-thing like that we'd all say yes — 'I know you're willing to be used, but are you willing *not* to be used? To have a *little* ministry? Are you willing for me to put you in a little corner and just keep you to myself?' And that was an altogether different question. I think it's one of the things the Lord dealt with me most about.

It's a command to be controlled. Every facet of my being, every area of my personality, that's the way we are filled with the Holy Spirit.

How is a person filled? I was amazed to find as I began to study the subject in the New Testament that the Bible doesn't tell us *how*. I used to think, well, you pray. You can do that, but I can't find any record of anybody literally praying in Scripture to be filled with the Spirit. They were praying on the day of Pentecost – but it doesn't say what for. Now I don't think it's wrong to pray to be filled – I believe we can – but I don't believe that's the way. In Acts 4, when they prayed – do you know what they prayed? The whole petition was, 'Grant unto thy servants that with all boldness we may speak thy word, and that signs and wonders may be done in the name of thy son, Jesus.' When they surrendered themselves to Jesus Christ, and all they wanted was his glory – *then* the Spirit of God fell!

Listen – the Holy Spirit has only one interest. He wants to glorify Jesus. I believe that when my desire matches his purpose, that's when I'm filled with the Holy Spirit. I may ask, I may not. But when all I want is to be controlled by the Lord and for my life to be used as a display case for Jesus' glory, I believe the Holy Spirit will fill me.

3. *It is a command to be controlled continually.* That's a present tense, 'Be filled with the Spirit', and he means 'Be *being* filled.' A continual fullness of the Spirit is to be a characteristic of the believer's life. You say, 'Is that possible?' I believe it is. The Bible isn't filled with 'impossible for man'. You say, 'That isn't possible.' Well it is, if God wants you to be filled. Did you know that every time God gives us a command he at the same time gives us the power to obey that

command? It will change your whole outlook if you turn all the commands into promises. That's why John can say 'His commands are not grievous' – they are not burdensome – because they are, literally, promises.

'Be ye being filled with the Spirit.' I believe there is the possibility in every Christian's life of being continually filled with the Spirit. That's why I asked the question at the beginning as I did. 'Is the Holy Spirit filling you' – present tense – 'right now?' Not, 'Has he filled you in the past?' It is possible, I believe, for us to live in a moment-by-moment surrender and submission to the Lord Jesus Christ. That does not mean 'perfection'. We are not free from sin, but we become so sensitive to the Spirit, so under the control of the Spirit, that immediately the Spirit of God convicts us, we do business with God. We confess and claim his forgiveness and cleansing, and we continue in the Spirit's fullness. I believe it's possible.

Paul says, 'Be ye being filled with the Spirit' and you'll notice that in the King James Version the next three verses all begin with participles. 'Speaking to yourselves', 'Giving thanks', and 'Submitting to one another' – I believe that these verses give us the conditions for continual fullness.

'Speaking to yourselves', he says in verse 19. 'Use your heart as a stringed instrument' – that's literally what he said! First of all, if I'm going to maintain the fullness of the Spirit, there must be joyful sharing with God's people. You cannot live a life of continual fullness if you're out of sorts with God's people – you just can't do it! 'Speaking to one another' – *sharing* with one another. The fullness of the Spirit takes the padlock off your mouth. There is a joyful worship with each other.

Secondly, he says in verse 20, 'Always giving thanks for all things in the name of our Lord Jesus Christ to God, even the Father'. What a statement! It means that even in the worst circumstances we recognise that our God is a sovereign God and he is in charge, and we give to him the praise and thanksgiving. Do you believe God is a sovereign God? I believe you do. My theology professor said that the sovereignty of God means simply this; 'God can do as he pleases and do it right well.' Now, when you and I begin to murmur and stop being thankful, we're simply accusing God of mis-management.

Thirdly, 'submitting yourselves to one another'. Mutual submission, service, helping the other person. Continually being filled with the Spirit by sharing with each other in worship, by continually recognising as God as Lord and thanking him in the midst of everything and by continually placing ourselves at the disposal of our fellow man to serve and help him in a Christ-like way.

This is being continually filled with the Spirit. Is the Spirit of God filling you right now? At this very moment, is the Holy Spirit filling you? Can you say, 'Lord, as best as I know how – as far as I am able to determine – there is nothing I'm withholding from the Lord and I, as best as I know how, am living in submission to his total will. I know the Spirit is filling me right now because he is in control. He can do with me as he pleases.'

THE STEWARDSHIP OF
THE GOSPEL'

by the Rev. Theodore Williams

It was said, a few years back, that note should be taken of the fact of the existence of a world-wide church. Today there is another fact of which we ought to take note, and that is the existence of a world-wide missionary movement. I was sharing something of what God is doing in India, at a missionary conference about seven years ago, and at the end of the meeting a lady said, 'If that is so, then why do we need to send missionaries there? There is so much to be done here.'

A very interesting question, one that perhaps comes naturally to many minds when we hear about missionaries going out of Asia or African or Latin-American countries. Why then *should* missionaries go to those places from England, Europe or America?

Just because there is a world-wide missionary movement today it does not mean that those who are sending missionaries should stop. There will always be the need to send missionaries from God's church everywhere to those who have not heard the Gospel everywhere; and this is not the time to talk about withdrawal, but to talk about an intelligent redeployment of forces, a wise use of resources and personnel in the spirit of international Christian partnership. This is what I'm pleading for. This is not the time to feel depressed or discouraged, nor is it the time to feel satisfied or complacent; it is certainly a time to feel excited and thrilled because of what God is doing. It is also a time to feel alert and to be discerning, to see how best we can use the resources at our disposal.

A word that comes to my mind on an occasion such as this is 'stewardship'; and I turn your attention to Paul's second letter to the Corinthians chapter 5. Here we will find the Pauline understanding of stewardship.

The moment we hear the word 'stewardship' in certain circles – and I speak here as a Methodist minister – we think of money. But the word is much more comprehensive. It does not only refer to money, and that is what we notice in 2 Corinthians 5. For instance, Paul speaks of the stewardship of the Gospel in verses 18 and 19.

All this is from God, who through Christ reconciled us to himself and gave us the ministry of reconciliation; that is, God was in Christ reconciling the world to himself, not counting their trespasses against them, and entrusting to us the message of reconciliation.

In the studies earlier in 1 Thessalonians we noticed how Paul speaks of this same stewardship, the stewardship of the Gospel. Here he says we have been given a message, the message of reconciliation. We have also been given the ministry of reconciliation. Call it the two sides of the Gospel coin. This is a message to proclaim: there is a ministry to perform. There is a service to render: there is a witness to speak of and to declare.

135

Together, these constitute the Gospel, and Paul says that the responsibility of the Gospel has been entrusted into our hands. Now what does this mean?

It certainly means that we have to guard the Gospel. Paul was overwhelmed with this sense of stewardship; see 1 Corinthians 9:16, 22–23, where he says that the stewardship of the Gospel not only enabled him to share the Gospel, but, in a sense, controlled his entire life. He's talking of a Gospel life-style, to which a stewardship of the Gospel must lead us. Friends, I find that today the greatest hindrance to the advance of the Gospel is that we have unnecessarily dichotomised the whole responsibility. We have said, 'Here are those who go. These are the heroes and heroines of missions. We will stand behind and admire them.'

They go to a country like Ethiopia with courage and daring, and there in faith they labour. They go to a country like Thailand, and are willing to be martyrs. They go to some other land with all opposition and bigotry and they face those difficulties. My, these are certainly the heroes and heroines of missions! We'll stand on the sidelines and applaud them, admire them, talk about their sacrifice and occasionally send some money to support them; but we are not those who would be there. They are the 'goers'. We are the 'senders'.

Now there is a separation in the call. Some are called to go and others are not. But as I read the Scriptures, apart from that call there is a separation or distinction in nothing else. When you take missionary concern, it is the same for all believers. When you take missionary involvement, it is the same for all believers. When you take missionary consecration, sacrifice or obedience, it is the same for all believers. You don't say that those who go are called to one standard of sacrifice and those who are not called to go are called to another standard. All God's people should have the same involvement, obedience, call to consecration and sacrifice. The only difference is the call. To some the Lord of the Harvest says, 'I want you there'; to others, 'I want you here.' So my whole life whether I live it here or there should be controlled by this one concern, that is, the Gospel must be advanced. That affects my values, my priorities, my goals, ambitions, recreation, amusements, social life; and because the church of Christ has not recognised this, there are many who have still not heard the Gospel.

Oh, for the company of those who are completely involved! This is the stewardship of the Gospel. And when I go through my own land of India this is what I say to our own church, and praise God, he is raising up people who are coming to realise this; that their whole life must be affected by the one concern, that the Gospel be taken to those who do not have it. Yes, the whole life must be lived in that consciousness. I'm not here just because God has not called me to be there, but as far as the passion, the willingness to sacrifice is concerned, the one who has gone and I who stay here are the same. This will save me from petty and trifling things, from things that dissipate my time and energy; and you know, there are Christians today who are preoccupied with things that do not matter. I think of a man on a tiger hunt. There he was sitting waiting, and under the tree he had tied a buffalo carcass as a bait. It was dark, and he was sitting, alert to every movement. And all of a sudden some mosquitoes gathered around and they started biting and he just laid his gun aside and started swatting the mosquitoes. And the tiger came and took the buffalo. That is the story of many

Christians today. God has called them to a greater task, but they are busy swatting mosquitoes. If there is a stewardship of the Gospel, dare we do that?

Then Paul speaks of a stewardship of people. 2 Corinthians 5:16; 'From now on, therefore, we regard no-one from a human point of view.' The word 'therefore' links it with the previous text. 'Therefore', because of the Cross, because Christ died and rose again, we do not regard anyone from a human point of view. In other words, he says, my whole perspective of people has changed. I look at people now through Calvary glasses, as those for whom Christ died and rose again. We are responsible for those who are near to us and live in our world. When we hear of their need of the Gospel we ought to be challenged. We're told that there are four billion people in the world today, of whom almost two and a half billion are often spoken of as 'untouched'. One fifth of those people live in my own country. Four hundred and twenty-five tribes in India, many of whom have never heard the Gospel, never heard the name of Jesus even once. A fifth of this world's population consists of Muslims, and there are Muslim countries today which are closed to the Gospel, where no preacher of the Gospel can get in.

In earlier days, some of the best men from the universities went out to witness among the Muslims. Where are such people today? The unreached of Islam still remain unreached. Are we no longer stewards of people? As long as there is one person who has not heard the name of Jesus, am I not responsible for that person? Yes, there is a stewardship of people. There are those who have never heard of Jesus even once.

I serve as the General Secretary of the Indian Evan-

gelical Mission. We are committed to reaching the unreached, mainly in India and also around India. We had
a medical doctor serving in one remote area. A tribal
woman came to her and asked for medicine. She gave
her the medicine and prayed for her. The next day the
woman came back, healed; she was so full of joy. She
didn't ask for more medicine, she asked for the name,
the name of Jesus. 'Tell me the name of the God in
whose name you prayed.' The doctor replied, 'Jesus'.
The woman kept repeating the name but could not
remember it. Can you believe it? Her mind was so
darkened. And she could not remember the name. The
missionary went on leave and returned after a month,
and the woman met her with a radiant face and said,
'I've been praying to your God.' 'How can you pray?'
asked the missionary. 'You don't even know his name.'
She said, 'I may not remember his name, but I know
him. I call him Baboo's God, your God, and that's how
I pray to him.'

They would believe in him only if they heard, but
they've not heard. Think of all that name means to you
this morning. The consolation, the courage, the hope,
the access that we have to the throne of our heavenly
Father, in that name. Imagine a people *without* that
name. There are many, many such. You know what
God's purpose is? It is that out of every group of people,
every nation, there should be a people for himself. He
does not look at this world as a collection of nations
who are on the list of the United Nations Organisation.
No, he is thinking more in terms of peoples identifiable
by language, culture, a way of life. In that sense India
is a land of many nations. And God's will is that from
among these pockets of people there must be a people
for himself. Am I identified with that purpose of God?

As long as there are unreached people of this world, how can I keep quiet?

I want to say to young people, the day of pioneering missionaries is not over. Don't let anybody tell you that the world has heard the Gospel. There is still need for adventure, still need for daring faith. May God grip us with this concern, that the people who have never heard the Gospel, wherever they may be, must hear it. Just because doors may be closed we have not been released from our commission. We are still bound, we are still committed.

Then lastly, Paul speaks in this passage of a stewardship of life. Verse 10: 'We must all appear before the judgement seat of Christ so that each one may receive good or evil according to what he has done in the body.' There will be a day of reckoning. We will have to give an account. And how careful we ought to be in the spending of our lives! Things that will not matter in eternity, do not matter now. Things which will matter intensely in eternity must matter now.

There is a stewardship of life. What are you going to do with that life? Some say, 'I'll just try it out', and sometimes it looks as if Jesus Christ is running an employment agency and we go to him with our list of qualifications and say, 'Now, Lord, please have a look at this and see if I fit in anywhere.' No. We must go to him and say, 'You are Lord of my life, where you send me I will go; what you want me to do I will do. My commitment is not necessarily to a place or to a job, but it is to you, and wherever you take me, I will follow.'

And if Jesus Christ is Lord, if he is Lord of my life and of this universe, as long as there are people who have not acknowledged him as Lord and King, I must be stirred to give my life into his hands.

And so the challenge of the missionary meeting this morning is a challenge to invest our lives in his hands. Whether he calls you to go or not is not the point. All lives must be given into his hands. He will decide whether we have to go or to stay, but the involvement is the same.

During the Second World War, Japan was winning many victories. One reason was the dedication of those who joined the Japanese army, airforce and navy. In the airforce there was a group called the *Kamikaze*, the 'divine winged pilots'; a suicide squad. The pilot would crash his plane, loaded with bombs, into the target. The plane would explode, the pilot die, but the target would be hit.

There was one ambition that fired the *Kamikaze*. We will not live to see it, they said, but one day our Emperor will be the Emperor of the whole world, and our flag will fly over the whole world. And for that we'll give our lives.

Jesus Christ must be the Lord of all peoples of the world. And he wants lives. This is stewardship.

MAINTAINING THE FULLNESS OF THE SPIRIT

by the Rev. Ken Prior

Our topic tonight is the matter of holiness, which is the supreme concern of the Holy Spirit, the Spirit of Holiness, and is the theme of the passage in which these little words come: 'Be filled with the Spirit.'

We ought to look briefly at the context. I think it's rather significant. You'll notice the atmosphere of the verses that follow, the 'addressing one another in psalms and hymns and spiritual songs, singing and making melody to the Lord with all your heart'. In other words we expect a person who is filled with the Spirit to be also someone who is filled with praise to God. He will want to sing with his fellow-Christians. And that, of course, is an emphasis that is often given. It's perfectly true, as you'll see from the passage. But, if you look at the verses that go before it, you see another, different kind of emphasis. There it is on a person who is thoughtful and careful. Notice the atmosphere there. There it is that a Christian is a thoughtful person, one using his mind and the wisdom God can give to that mind. He is also disciplined, and in particular in the use of time, which is perhaps the most strategic matter over which we need to be disciplined in our lives. Then, of course, he is not only disciplined but guided. He is not foolish but he comes to understand – notice that word to do with the mind again – what the will of the Lord is.

And so we might expect a Spirit-filled Christian to have both kinds of property in his life. Without the fervour of the psalms, hymns and spiritual songs, a person would be a very dull and lifeless person; on the other hand, if you have the fervour without the thought and the discipline and the care, you would be a very shallow person. And a person who is filled with the Spirit is going to avoid both those extremes and is surely going to know the balance that this particular paragraph represents.

Now to the actual words themselves. One of the great difficulties of studying these particular thoughts is that they don't come all that frequently in Scripture and here we have to rely a great deal on the actual language that is used. Here are a series of steps that I want you to follow through with me as we try to penetrate what is in the apostle's mind as he uses these words.

1. *Here is a general command addressed to every Christian*. Firstly, it is a *command to obey*, rather than an experience to seek. No question about that. 'Be filled with the Spirit', is what the apostle says here. Now the other times that you find this idea of the fullness of the Spirit in Scripture, it does not come as a command. Take just one or two examples. In Acts 2, we are told that on the day of Pentecost they were all filled with the Spirit. Here was something that happened in the sovereignty of God. There was nothing that they were called on to do except, following the resurrection and ascension, to wait for this promise that God had given.

That is what they did and that was what then happened: 'They were filled.' It's given as a statement of something that happened; and it's repeated again in Acts 4. Of course it is open to God to break in in this way whenever it pleases him and his sovereign will. But notice, when you turn to what Paul says in Ephesians 5, it is a command given to us to obey.

Then, it is *a general command*. Let me explain what I mean by that. You see sometimes you'll find that being filled with the Spirit seems to have been to meet the demands of a special occasion; for example, in witness, or in facing opposition. Acts 4:8; 'Then Peter, filled with the Holy Spirit, said to them . . . ' It seems that the Holy Spirit came upon him for the particular demands and challenge he was facing. And there are many examples of that in history, and I have no doubt that many of us could testify to that. But you see, in the text here it is not only a command but it is a general command; not just for a particular occasion because literally it means 'go on being filled'. It's a present imperative. It describes a condition which is here placed before us as needed.

So, it is a command, it is a general command – and it is *a command addressed to every Christian*. It could be argued that those in the Acts of the Apostles were very special people. Barnabas, for example, was a good man, full of the Holy Spirit and of faith. But Barnabas was a special person, you might say. But you see, one can't get round it that way when faced with this command of the apostle, because Paul is addressing not just the leaders in Ephesus, he's addressing all of them. Notice that Paul is writing a general epistle. He's not, as far as we can gather, writing to any particular constituency, so we can't say that this applies to any particular kind of need. It's addressed to every Christian. Now here of course we contrast the so-called gifts – the 'charismata' – where we are told in Romans 12, I Corinthians 12 and so on, that the sovereign Spirit gives different gifts to different people. But here is a command addressed to every Christian.

2. *This is normal Christian experience.* Let me explain what I mean by that. Some people talk like this: 'Our minister hardly ever speaks about the fullness of the Holy Spirit' – and it's meant as a criticism. Do you know, you could level exactly the same thing at the apostle Paul? If this is a general command for every Christian, why do you only find it here? What about the Romans, the Corinthians, the Galatians, the Philippians and so on – after all, there was a lot wrong with many of them, which is quite clear from the letters; surely being filled with the Spirit would have been the answer. And then, what about the other New Testament writers ¬ James, Peter, John? Did they never use this expression? Apparently not; certainly not in the letters we have in the New Testament. Now why should this be? One of the troubles is that there's a misunderstanding that it's easy to fall into.

The fact is this. You cannot separate the persons of the Trinity. They don't act independently of each other. For example, in Romans 8:9, the Holy Spirit is called, within one verse, 'the Spirit', 'the Spirit of God', and 'the Spirit of Christ'. When, earlier in this very epistle (Ephesians 3:19) Paul says 'that you may be filled with all the fullness of God', isn't that only through being filled by the indwelling Spirit? And if you'll look back at the verses that go before that, you'll find it's so. And then isn't this how Jesus himself foresaw the work of the Holy Spirit, in the midst of those great chapters, John 14–16? Notice the ways he expresses it. He says that the Counsellor, the Comforter will be in you. In another verse Jesus refers to him by saying 'I will be in you', and yet again, 'If a man loves me he will keep my word, and my Father will love him and *we* will come to him and will make our home with him.' When Charles Wesley wrote that great hymn,

> My heart is full of Christ, and longs
> Its glorious matter to declare . . .

is that any different from being filled by the Holy Spirit who is the Spirit of Christ? You see, there are various ways of expressing the fullness of the Holy Spirit without necessarily using this exact word. One of the very first things Paul says, when he is writing to the Ephesians, is that 'in Christ we have been blessed with all spiritual blessings' (1:3). He says something very similar to the Colossians (2:9–10): 'In him' – that is, in Christ – 'the whole fullness of Deity dwells' – and so verse 10 follows with inevitable logic, 'and you have come to fullness of life in him.'

If you receive Christ, and in Christ all the fullness of Deity dwells, how could you possibly have Christ without having the Holy Spirit – and the Holy Spirit in all his fullness, at that? So you see what Paul is doing here is facing the Ephesians with something which they already have in the purposes of God, and the great danger is not only that they fail to go on to something extra but that they fall away from what is the basic, initial promise of the Gospel.

So let's come and ask ourselves the question: 'How do you actually fulfil a command like this?' Because it's in the passive. How do you fulfil a passive command?

Suppose I said to you, 'Be touched by that person over there', how would you set about obeying me? You cannot. Unless, and this is the basic pre-supposition of a passive command, the person over there is already attempting to touch you. What I'm really saying to you is, 'Don't jump out of the way; don't prevent him; allow him.'

And this seems to me to be why the New English Bible has hit on what seems to me to be the best way to express a passive command: 'Let the Holy Spirit fill you.' In other words, what we are called to do is not just to do something, to initiate something, but to allow the Holy Spirit to do something *he* wants to do. And what is that? Literally, it is ' . . . filled *in* the Spirit . . . '

That's not quite how some people see it. Some of us tend to think of the Holy Spirit as a kind of liquid and we as empty vessels that need filling up. Now, of course the Holy Spirit is spoken of as a liquid, especially as a flowing river, but the Holy Spirit is something more than a liquid. He is a person. So we could say, 'Be filled – know a life of fullness – with regard to the Holy Spirit'; or, to put it another way, 'Be controlled by the Spirit; be under his influence.'

And here you see the significance of the contrast in this verse. 'Drunk with wine' means to be under the influence of wine. We sometimes speak of somebody being under the influence of strong drink; and that, says Paul, is debauchery. The word is translated as 'riotous', describing the Prodigal Son in Luke 15. It means the opposite of 'to save'; it means 'to throw away' or 'to waste', and so it involves a lack of self-control.

Instead, the apostle says, be controlled by the Spirit; let the Holy Spirit fill, control you. Now what is it that Holy Spirit seeking to do? If it's just a matter of not standing in his way, what does he want to do? Here we have to look very much behind what the apostle is saying, and a very helpful thing to do is to put Ephesians 5 alongside Colossians 3. Paul wrote these epistles at about the same time and so he uses similar language as well as similar material. Sometimes, in fact, the language is identical. And this passage from the Ephesians 5 has its equivalent in Colossians 3 which is similar and sometimes identical. But when you come to the expression ' . . . be filled with the Spirit', you'll find in Colossians there's something different. Colossians 3:16–17; 'Let the word of Christ dwell in you richly . . . ' In other words, Paul can substitute one for the other. They're two sides of the same coin. Now is this a fluke, or does something lie behind it?

Let me give you just a brief glance of what lies behind it. Right at the beginning of Scripture, the Spirit of God was moving on the face of the water (Genesis 1:2), and, verse 3, 'God said, "Let there be . . . " ' The Spirit of God, and the word of God. One could go right through Scripture, seeing the way 'word' and 'Spirit' come together. But for the present the most significant way is the way in which the New Testament age is foreseen. In Ezekiel, the new covenant contains the promise of a new heart and a new spirit (it's debatable whether the 's' should be a capital or not, but there's no doubt that the way God gives us a new spirit is by the indwelling of his Holy Spirit). When you turn to Jeremiah, for example 31:31–34, you have one of the distinctive features of the new covenant as follows: ' . . . I will put' – not my *Spirit*, but – 'my Law within them, and I will write it on their hearts.'

Now, when you come to Paul (2 Corinthians 3:3) you'll find him bringing these two thoughts together.

He describes his readers as 'a letter from Christ delivered by us, written not with ink but with the Spirit of the living God, not on tablets of stone but on tablets of human hearts.' In other words; Christ writes, and his ink is the Holy Spirit. And so we could go on and see the same thing through Paul's writings. You see, they're the same truth.

So what is the Holy Spirit seeking to promote? God's Law on our hearts. Notice that he is not seeking that we should outwardly imitate the Law of God. The sanctifying work of the Spirit is an inward work and his intention is that we should want to obey God's word and Law as part of our inward nature.

And the supreme example of that in practice is of course the Lord Jesus. What was his instinctive reaction to the temptations of the devil, in the wilderness? 'It is written . . . ' So you see what God is seeking to do. As we study the word of God and seek to obey it, his purpose is that his Holy Spirit will be writing it on our hearts.

And now we come to the final question. If this is the Holy Spirit's purpose, what is preventing him? What is the great antagonist of the Spirit in the New Testament? There's a word the apostle uses again and again, and that's 'flesh'. It can be translated 'self'. Who is it that prevents the Holy Spirit from doing what he wants? Y-O-U! That's all.

The great call of God from these five little words is this. What God calls upon us to do is not just something of our own initiative; not just to plan and purpose some great thing; but to give way to what he wants to do – and that command is a continuous one. Not only now, but every day. When we're faced with trying circumstances, when our temper starts to rise – that's the moment when we let the Holy Spirit control, because the only alternative is to let self do what it wants to do. Not just now, but tomorrow, in our family life, in our place of work, in every situation.

If it doesn't only apply now, however, it certainly includes now. And what God is saying now with his word is, 'What is holding the Holy Spirit back from controlling you? It's the great alternative. It's either what *I* want to do, or whether I let the Holy Spirit control. And that is what God calls us to do.

There are many things to discover in the Christian life, many truths to discover, and a wonderful pattern of life we're told to follow; but here Paul, in the midst of a very practical passage, tells us that one of the basic things we need to do is to be filled with the Spirit – let the Holy Spirit control.

THE EFFECTS OF THE FULLNESS

by the Rev. Gilbert Kirby

If you've been around for some time, as I have, you'll
find that fashions change. And this applies to theology,
strangely enough. Emphases change. In my younger
days people used to say that the Holy Spirit was the most
neglected person of the Trinity. I'm almost inclined to
say that you hardly hear about anything else these days.
We've gone full circle from neglecting the Holy Spirit to
almost becoming obsessed with him. Now, thank God
for the gift of the Holy Spirit; thank God for the
Holy Spirit. Had it not been for the Holy Spirit you
would not be a Christian; because you were born again
of the Spirit, you are indwelt by the Spirit, you are
gifted by the Spirit for Christian service, you are enabled by the Spirit for Christian work and witness.

Now, how would you expect to recognise a Spirit-filled
Christian? Think of that. Would he be singing all the
time. Would he have a huge badge saying: 'Smile, Jesus
loves you'? Well, he might; but neither of those would
be a clear indication of whether he or she was filled by
the Holy Spirit of God. Now the Bible always brings

us down to earth; and I delight to bring to you now a very practical message. What does being filled with the Holy Spirit mean in practical terms? How does it affect our lives?

We find, first of all, that *being filled with the Spirit affects our worship*. We are told to 'address one another in psalms and hymns and spiritual songs, singing and making melody to the Lord with all your heart, always and for everything giving thanks in the name of our Lord Jesus Christ to God the Father.' Worship is no longer a dull and monotonous duty. It is now a spiritual delight. Worship is now meaningful, and, my friends, this is something that some of us still have to learn – the place of worship in our lives.

God delights in the worship of his people. Worship is a spiritual activity. Now, I believe in the value of preaching, of course, but never let preaching oust worship from its rightful place in our lives. How do we worship? Well, it mentions here psalms and hymns and spiritual songs. I think we neglect the psalms to our great loss. Here is our natural worship manual. It was the manual of the Jews and we, their spiritual successors, should delight to use the psalms in worship. You can take almost any psalm and it leads you into a spirit of worship. And of course hymns, good hymns – thank God for them and for the writers of them. And spiritual songs – I dare to suggest that we might almost equate those with choruses – yes, but choruses with a difference. I thank God for the new kind of chorus that has come into our vocabulary because it's scriptural and therefore more spiritual than many of the choruses I sang in my youth: 'I am H-A-P-P-Y, I know I am, I'm sure I am, I'm H-A-P-P-Y.' Well, I suppose it's all right for tiny tots but there's not much theology in it, and there's certainly hardly any Christianity in it. But there *are* spiritual songs, and these are to be used in our worship to the glory of God.

It goes on to say that in our worship we give thanks for everything in the name of our Lord Jesus Christ. We are filled with the Spirit of God and we are a grateful people for all God's blessings to us and all the benefits that we've inherited through our Lord and Saviour Jesus Christ. Isn't worship something that is going to be the hallmark of a Spirit-filled believer? A person who loves to worship, not a person who sits in a pew and mechanically goes through a form but someone who enters into the spirit of worship, who thinks what he's doing, follows the prayers, and sings the hymns meaningfully. If they are spiritual hymns, inspired by the Spirit of God, then they are instruments of worship which we delight to use. So there's one very definite hallmark of a Spirit-filled Christian; someone who loves to worship God with his heart and soul and not merely as a mechanical exercise.

Now I'm sure you'll go with me on that, but I almost tremble to mention the other hallmark of a Spirit-filled believer. Overall *the outstanding characteristic of a Spirit-filled believer can be summed up in just one word: submissive.* Oh, you say, how tame! I don't like that. No, you won't like it. But if a man or a woman is filled with the Spirit of God there is about them a new submissiveness. Maybe that person before was bossy, domineering, self-appointed, seeking their own glory. I once saw a motto card in a shop window and it said on it: 'The door to success is marked "Push".' Can you think of anything less spiritual, less Christian, than that? That is the wisdom of the world. But I tell you, from the Scriptures, that the hallmark of a Spirit-filled

Christian is a submissive spirit.

Look at Ephesians 5:21, 'Be submissive to one another out of reverence for Christ' – out of respect for Christ, if you like, bearing in mind the Spirit and the mind of he who ' . . . though he was rich yet for our sakes became poor . . . ' I love that Christological passage, don't you, in Philippians 2. It says: 'Have this mind in you which you have in Christ Jesus, who, though he was in the form of God, thought it not a thing to be grasped at to be equal with God, but emptied himself . . . ' (or, as the Authorised Version puts it: ' . . . made himself of no reputation . . . ') He submitted himself. 'I am meek and lowly . . . ' Now that doesn't come naturally to most people. Most people, beneath the surface, are pretty self-assertive; but when a man or a woman is filled with the Spirit of God you see in them a new submissiveness; they're not always standing up and laying down the law, like 'Diotrephes, who loves to have the pre-eminence'. You can imagine him at a church meeting – first one on his feet if he'd got anything to say or not. Just imagine the poor man in the chair, trying to deal with a fellow like that. You see, that's not the Spirit of Christ; submissiveness is.

Now it's easy to talk in general terms, isn't it? You see, it only comes home to us when we localise it in specific situations. And this general submissiveness, which should be the hallmark of all Christians, has to be worked out in concrete situations. The apostle Paul gives us three, and at least one of them will apply to most people here.

There is *the submissiveness of a wife to her husband.* Yes, I know about Women's Lib. It isn't doing womanhood any good; it's doing a great disservice to the women of our country. Without wanting to give offence, I suppose American society is the most matriarchal in the world, but it's also the society that produces the most divorces. Marriage was instituted by God; God made man and woman; he made them to be complementary to one another and in his purposes he ordained that for a successful marriage man must take the lead and be the final responsible person and woman must submit to that situation. Clearly there is, according to the Scripture, a place for submissiveness within the marriage relationship and I don't see how, with Scripture open before us, we can possibly deny that.

Now let's come to another area which isn't very popular either; *submissiveness in the home.* 'Children, obey your parents in the Lord, for this is right. Honour your father and mother . . . ' (this is the first commandment with a promise) ' . . . that it may be well with you and that you may live long on the earth.' What an unpopular doctrine! Oh, you say, that's Victorian. No, it isn't; it's scriptural. It just happens to be New Testament Christianity. And what has happened? As we've moved away from that commandment our Juvenile Courts have filled up with youngsters beyond parental control; we have juvenile delinquency on an unprecedented scale because we have forgotten God's ordering of things.

Now I'm interested to read in the Old Testament that Eli was judged, through Samuel, because his sons were blaspheming God and he did not restrain them; I'm interested to read verse after verse in the book of Proverbs in effect saying, 'Spare the rod and spoil the child'; I'm interested to read that in the New Testament church one of the conditions for a leader, an elder, an overseer, was that he should be someone who could manage his own household well, keeping his children submissive and respectful in every way. In other words, if you didn't keep the commandment – you didn't bring your children up to be submissive – you automatically forfeited the right to be a Christian leader. I wonder how many would have to resign from eldership, or being deacons, or from parochial church councils if we took seriously that condition of leadership.

Submissiveness within the marriage relationship, submissiveness within the home and then (and it's really quite as unpopular as the rest) *submissiveness at work*. Well, you say, you're taking us back, surely, to the beginning of the century, if not before. No, I'm not; I'm taking you back to Scripture. I know we don't have slaves today, but we do have employees; and I would say that the principle applies here even though the actual momenclature is different. Employees ' . . . be obedient to those who are your earthly masters, with fear and trembling, in singleness of heart, as to Christ; not in the way of eyeservice as men-pleasers, but as servants of Christ, doing the will of God from the heart, rendering service with a good will as to the Lord and not to men, knowing that whatever good any one does, he will receive the same again from the Lord, whether he is a slave or free.' In other words, you expect a Spirit-filled Christian to be a loyal worker doing the very best he can for his boss, doing it with singleness of heart, as though he were working for the Lord himself, and not doing it just because he's being watched by the manager or the foreman. How do you measure up to that? Are you a Spirit-filled Christian? Well, what's the evidence?

But let's be fair – that's not the whole story. Submissiveness on the one hand and considerateness or consideration on the other. What about being considerate as a husband? A Spirit-filled husband is going to love his wife ' . . . as Christ loved the church and gave himself up for her'. Now could you be more considerate than that? That's what it says: ' . . . let each one of you love his wife as himself . . . ' Now submissiveness is no problem if consideration is at that level. I was intrigued to run across a verse in Peter 3:7; 'Likewise, you husbands, live considerately with your wives, bestowing honour on the woman as the weaker sex, since you are joint heirs of the grace of life, in order that your prayers may not be hindered.' Have you ever thought, husbands with unconverted wives, have you ever thought that possibly your prayers have not been answered because you're not a nice enough, gracious enough, self-sacrificing enough husband? It may be that's why your prayers are not being answered. Yes, considerateness, or consideration, on the part of husbands to their wives.

Consideration on the part of parents to their children. 'Fathers, do not provoke your children to anger, but bring them up in the discipline and instruction of the Lord.' ' . . . do not provoke your children to anger . . . ' Don't nag them; don't keep on at them; don't irritate them unnecessarily; leave them alone sometimes. Considerateness for your children. Don't be harsh. There's one thing in being strong, and a true parent; it's quite another thing to be unkind and harsh.

And then, what about the slave and master situation, or the employee and employer situation? 'Masters, do the same to them . . . ' In other words, show them the same consideration ' . . . and forbear threatening, knowing that he who is both their Master and yours is in heaven and that there is no partiality with him.' Masters, don't be hard taskmasters. You expect your servants, your employee, to be submissive to you but

157

be worthy of their submission.

Now, how can you tell Spirit-filled Christians? They've got a happy marriage; they've worked it out on scriptural principles. It's no good you saying to me you're a Spirit-filled Christian, you wife, if you're constantly bossing your husband – you didn't find that in scripture. It's no good you saying to me that you're a Spirit-filled Christian, you husband, if you neglect your wife, never take her out, never think of her interests, never go out of your way to show love for her – you don't find that in Scripture. It's no good you telling me you're a Spirit-filled Christian father or mother, if you don't take the trouble to bring your children up in the nurture and admonition of the Lord, if you're always out at meetings – yes, spiritual meetings, so-called – when you ought to be looking after them and bringing them up and showing love to them. It's no good as a young person, especially if you're in your teens and feeling a bit rebellious, saying you've been filled with the Spirit of God if you take no notice of your parents, neglect them, show no respect for them. It's no good, you employee, going back to work perhaps on Monday, if you're always stirring up trouble, being disloyal to the firm, stirring it up, you know; that's not the mark of a Spirit-filled Christian. It's no good you, Boss, if you can't keep your employees, if there's a constant change-over because people can't work with you. I know, sad to say, Christians who have a terrible reputation for keeping people in their employ because, you see, there's no consideration.

When we talk and think about the fullness of the Spirit, we mustn't divide between doctrine and life – what we believe and how we behave. Perhaps you are very clear about what you believe about the Holy Spirit and the command that there is, to be being filled with the Holy Spirit. It may be that at one time you thought that meant that you were going to sing a lot more than you do now, you were going to get excited. Well, that's all right within measure, but it also means that you're going to live at a very different level in your home, with your family, your children; it means that you're going to have a different attitude to your work and to your employees or to your employer, as the case may be.

That is what it means to be filled with the Spirit. It's to work it out in everyday life. And you see, there's no sort of *carte blanche* – saying, 'Yes, right, from this moment . . . ' You've got to be 'being filled' with the Spirit. Everyday you've got to bring these things up before you, as it were, and before the Lord, and be filled as you go off to work, as you tackle your family problems. You've got to say, 'If I'm filled with the Spirit I'm going to be submissive' – to those around you, at home or at work, and above all, to the Lord.

THE LORDSHIP OF JESUS CHRIST

by the Rev. John Stott

If I were to ask you what is the really master-key doctrine, I wonder what you would answer. It would be very interesting if we could sit down and compare notes with one another. Some of you no doubt would say, the Sovereignty of God. Others, the Cross of our Lord Jesus Christ. Others would say, the Fullness of the Holy Spirit. And I would agree that they are all vital, central doctrines. But I want to argue that the master-key is somewhere else. It is in the Lordship of Christy.

I believe that the key Christian doctrine is in the affirmation 'Jesus Christ is Lord', and if that isn't central in our Christian belief, behaviour and experience then I think something is out of gear. But if we do see and acknowledge Jesus as Lord, then all our Christian doctrine and behaviour and experience mesh in with one another and we have found the integrating secret of the Christian life. I honestly believe that; I hope I may demonstrate it biblically, that the Lordship of Jesus is a wonderfully liberating doctrine. It is when Jesus is Lord that we are made whole and free.

1. *Our relationship to the Lord (Romans 14: 7–9).*
Let me suggest in the first place, when we acknowledge
Jesus as Lord, our relationship to him is right. The
alternatives are clearly set before us in verses 7, 8: 'None
of us lives to himself, none of dies to himself', and 'If
we live we live to the Lord, if we die we die to the Lord.'
That's the alternative. We're all either living to ourselves or living to the Lord. Of course the 'us' and the
'we' there mean Christians, because non-Christians are
doing exactly what verse 7 says 'none of us' does, that is,
they are living and dying to themselves. That is what it
means to be a non-Christian. It is to be self-centred, self-
absorbed, self-obsessed. That's what we are till Jesus
liberates us. But it's inconceivable that a Christian should
live like that. You see the whole of our human experience centres on Jesus Christ. Nothing, if we're Christians, is outside the sphere of his dominion. How is that?
Verse 9: 'To this end Christ died and lived again in order
that he might be . . . ' What? Supposing you didn't know
that verse, and I'd said, now, fill in the blank. Ninety-
nine out of a hundred would say 'Saviour'. Isn't that why
he died, and rose again, to be our Saviour? But it's not
what Paul said. He said, ' . . . that he might be Lord.'

The idea still lingers in some circles that it is possible
to accept Jesus as your Saviour and postpone indefinitely
the question of his Lordship. That is a preposterous idea.
The New Testament knows nothing of such bogus
Christianity. There is only one Jesus Christ, he is our
Lord and Saviour Jesus Christ; and response to Jesus
is response to the totality of Jesus our Saviour and Lord.
It's inconceivable that we should cut him up and respond
to only part of him. You can't. He can only *be* our
Saviour because he is Lord. It's from that position at the

Father's right hand that he justifies the believing sinner and bestows the Holy Spirit upon us; because he has the authority to do so. Let's not separate what God has joined or contradict the purpose for which Jesus has died and risen again. He's died and risen again in order that he might be Lord of both the dead and the living.

He's certainly the Lord of the Christian dead. In heaven, you know, the Christian dead give no grudging acquiescence to the Lordship of Jesus. There's only a joyful wondering adoration that Jesus Christ is Lord, the Lamb upon his throne. But he died and rose again not only to be Lord of the dead but of the living. He means our Christian life on earth to approximate as far as possible the glorified life of the believer in heaven. And that means a totality of surrender, to the Lordship of Jesus, joyful, ungrudging, wondering, total allegiance to Jesus. That includes everything, my friends; everything, you name it, it's under the Lordship of Jesus. When we acknowledge Jesus as Lord then our relationship to him is right.

2. *Our relationship to one another (Romans 14)*. Secondly, when we acknowledge Jesus as Lord our relationship to one another is right. Do you know Romans 14? It's mostly about the 'weaker brother'. The weaker brother is the Christian with a weak under-developed and over-sensitive conscience. In the church or churches in Rome there were Christians with a weak conscience and those with a strong conscience. One of the issues was whether Christians were allowed to eat meat. Those with a strong conscience felt perfectly at liberty to eat it, but those with a weak one felt they shouldn't and became vegetarians. Again, some regard some days as better and more important than others,

and other people regarded all days as alike. So you see in the church at Rome there was difference of opinion about certain foods and days.

Well, there's nothing wrong in differences of opinion about these minor matters. Of course we must be agreed about the major doctrines and all the fundamentals of the faith. But there's no reason why we shouldn't differ about minor matters; nothing wrong in that. Let's face reality: we're not going to agree with one another totally until we get to heaven, and Christians have got to learn to be tolerant of one another in the Christian family. After all, in the human family we learn to tolerate one another's idiosyncracies, don't we?

What disturbed the apostle Paul was not the existence of minor differences but the attitudes the Christians had to one another on account of their differences. They despised one another, they sat in judgement on one another (verses 2, 3). Let's understand this. What is Paul saying? How does he deal with the situation in the church at Rome? He deals with it theologically. He doesn't just appeal to those Roman Christians to be nice and kind and tolerant. No, he reminds them of a doctrine which they had forgotten or weren't applying to their situation.

We have no business to despise one another, no business to stand in judgement on the servants of Christ (verse 4). Again, don't let's misunderstand this. Paul considered some opinions to be false. For example, he was not a vegetarian and he didn't see any reason why he shouldn't eat meat that had been offered in sacrifice to idols. He knew that idols were nothing, they didn't exist. He could eat such meat with thanksgiving without any scruples at all. But, you remember, he would refrain, he would voluntarily curb his own liberty of conscience in the presence of a weak brother or sister, because it might cause them to do something against their conscience. If you do that you're sinning, and Paul didn't want them to do that, even if their conscience was mistaken. Scripture has a very high view of the human conscience. And when a conscience is weak and uneducated, it must still be respected.

Now the secret then of our relations with one another in the Christian church, especially when we have differences, is 'Jesus Christ is Lord'. To despise or stand in judgement on a fellow-Christian isn't just a breach of fellowship. It is a denial of the Lord Jesus. It is a presumptuous attempt to usurp Christ's prerogative as Lord. I need to say to myself, who am I, that I should cast myself in the role of another Christian's lord and judge? I must be willing for Jesus Christ to be not only my, but also my fellow-Christians', Lord and Judge. They are responsible to him and I must not interfere with Christ's lordship over other Christians. Do you know, our fellowship in the local church would be immediately sweetened and tension lightened if we were prepared to 'let other Christians go' – they're not responsible to us. I'm not their lord and judge; you're not my lord and judge. It's before him that we stand or fall. And if we acknowledge Jesus as Lord then immediately our relations with other people, with one another in the fellowship of the church, are put right.

3. *Our relationship to the outside world.* If we acknowledge Jesus as Lord then our relationship with the world outside is right as well; that is, the secular, the unbelieving, the Christ-rejecting world. Look on to verse 11. It's a favourite from Isaiah that Paul quotes on several occasions. The context here (verses 10, 12) is judgement. Each of us is going to give an account of

himself to Christ the Lord and Christ the Judge, and we mustn't therefore be lords and judges of each other. Nevertheless these words have a wider implication, justified because Paul uses the verse in other senses elsewhere. It is a quotation from Isaiah 45:22, 23. It's a wonderful missionary verse in the Old Testament, an astonishing flash of conviction that one day all the nations – not just Israel – are going to be included in the purpose of God, and in his best known use of this verse Paul applies it to Jesus.

In Philippians 2:9,10 Paul says that God has exalted Jesus so that at his name 'every knee shall bow and every tongue confess that Jesus Christ is Lord'. So what then is the supreme missionary motivation? It's not obedience to the Great Commission, or even love for a lost and lonely world, important as these are. It's the universal Lordship of Jesus. God has exalted Jesus and enthroned him at his right hand. God has given him universal authority over all nations, hence the affirmation of the risen Lord in Matthew 28:18. Exactly! and God's purpose in doing this is that every knee should bow to Jesus and every tongue confess him Lord. We should be full of indignation and jealousy for the honour and glory of Jesus Christ, and we should be full of restless energy to go and make him known. When we acknowledge Jesus as Lord, our relationship to the outside world is right.

So let me summarise. God has made Jesus Lord of all by creation, and also by his death and resurrection and ascension and enthronement at the right hand of God. Universal authority has been given to Jesus, he is Lord as a divine fact, and he is the undisputed Lord of the Christian dead for they ceaselessly worship him in heaven. So it's only on earth (if we leave aside the demons) that there are millions still withholding from Jesus the honour that is due to his name. And yet he died and rose again to this end, that he might be the Lord 'both of the dead and the living'. So I want to ask, did Jesus die and rise in vain, as far as we are concerned?

I began by suggesting that this is the key doctrine, the Lordship of Jesus. It's like the last piece of the jigsaw, the keystone in the arch, the final digit in the combination lock. If we acknowledge Jesus as Lord, everything else fits into place. Our relationships to him, to one another, and to the world, are put right.

So I end with some personal questions. Is Jesus Christ your Lord? Or are you denying his lordship in some way? To reject his teaching, to disobey his moral commandments, to rebel against his providential will, are all to deny the lordship of Jesus. To boss other Christians around and try to control them, to despise or stand in judgement on fellow-Christians – these are to deny the lordship of Jesus. To care, and do, nothing about the Christian mission in areas of the world where he is not acknowledged is to deny his lordship. And to deny the lordship of Jesus in any respect is to set ourselves against the purpose for which he died and rose again, for to this end he died and rose again: that he might be Lord both of the living and the dead.

Will you surrender to him that thing you have been withholding for years, whatever it be? For Jesus said, 'If you come after me you must take up your cross every day and follow me.' To deny his lordship is to skulk around in the darkness of fantasy. To acknowledge that Jesus is Lord is to come out into the sunshine of reality and then to go out and be the embodiment of my text tonight.

WALKING BY FAITH

by the Rev. Michael Fox

The lads at the school where I teach find themselves fascinated by the fact that I'm both a teacher and a clergyman. When one of them heard the other day that I was going to preach, he said, 'What are you going to preach about? God, or real life?' 'Both,' I said, and that's what I want to do tonight. I want to talk about walking by faith, and to do that we're going to look together at the example of Abraham.

Another lad in an R.E. lesson at school said seriously, 'I do believe . . . yet I wish I had a faith which was more sure.' He was only eleven. 'I wish I'd been there to see Jesus.' There was a stillness came upon the classroom as he said that. He'd got them thinking. And I suspect that this desire, like that of the father of the epileptic boy in Mark 9, is echoed by many, many Christians today. And I think the key problem for many of us, in our churches, at home, is: how do we translate our belief into trust? How can we get the faith in our heads to work out in experience?

Once I was a member of a church that had fallen on

hard times. Numbers were low. There were troubles in the choir. And sometimes on Sundays we used to sing a hymn by Wesley,

> Faith, mighty faith, the promise sees
> And looks to that alone;
> Laughs at impossibilities
> And cries, 'It shall be done.'[3]

And on Mondays and the rest of the week, we used to have endless debates, getting deeper and deeper into depression and gloom, about what was wrong with the church.

Do you remember how, in that story in Mark 9 about the epileptic boy, the disciples couldn't heal, Jesus arrived on the scene of their failure and – what did he find them doing? Praying? No. Silently repenting in shame over their failure to heal the boy? No. Verse 16: 'He found them having a discussion.'

I believe the church is bedevilled by discussion. Endless debates, synods, groups, words . . . words . . . words. Of course you've got to talk, but maybe it would be good to put up on the wall of the committee room 1 Corinthians 4:20; 'The kingdom of God does not consist in talk, but in power.' And power comes by faith in the God of power.

Now, according to the Bible, the supreme example of human faith is Abraham. 'Oh, no, I could never have Abraham's faith!' you may say. I don't know if you read those, what I call, Christian success books which keep appearing. I find myself saying, 'Well it never seems to work out like that for me.' What we need is not Abraham's faith but Abraham's God.

Do you know Romans 15:4? 'Whatever was written in former days was written for our instruction that by steadfastness and by the encouragement of the scriptures we might have hope.' So, we're going to study Abraham to be encouraged to have faith and hope renewed, and there are three simple things I want to say.

1. *Abraham's faith rested on the word of God.* Listen to Stephen's speech from Acts 7:5. 'God gave Abraham no inheritance in [Canaan], not even a foot's length, but promised to give it to him in possession and to his posterity after him, though he had no child.' God appeared, God spoke. Abraham had a revelation of God and heard God's voice.

I've no clear idea *how* – Genesis 15 talks about a vision – but the how doesn't matter, the fact is that God did appear and speak and he gave Abraham the double promise. And what was Abraham's response? He believed, and he obeyed. It's a classic example of faith, because Christian faith is always a response flowing from God's word.

Do you remember in John 20, how eight days after Easter Day. Jesus appeared to Doubting Thomas? And he spoke to him, and said, 'Come on, here I am, put your finger there' – and Thomas believed. He had seen Jesus, heard the words, and believed. And then John, after writing the story, says, 'These words and works of Jesus are written that *you* may believe.' Faith comes from the word of God.

Christian faith can't be 'worked up'. You'll remember the White Queen in *Alice through the Looking Glass*, who said to Alice, 'why, sometimes I've believed as many as six impossible things before breakfast!' That's nothing like true Christian faith. Christian faith is a response to God's self-revelation.

Abraham's faith *rested* on the word of God. It didn't

alight on it like a butterfly and then take off again. He kept on trusting. Hebrews 6:15; 'Abraham, having patiently endured, obtained the promise.' Well, it was twenty-five years before Isaac was born. We Christians so often want results from God on demand. Not so.

Notice another thing about Abraham and his faith. He looked problems in the face. He was a realist, not an escapist, as we see in Romans 4:19. True faith looks steadily at God's promises and is not put off by delay and apparent impossibilities.

2. *Abraham's faith made him ready to take risks.* The test of faith, surely, is what are you prepared to stake on the one you say you trust? How much will you risk?

When my grandfather was a young man he was approached by a man named Smith, who wanted him to put up two hundred pounds for a project. Grandad said, 'Well, what's the project?' So Mr Smith said, 'I'm going to do things with potatoes. Two hundred pounds – will you take the risk?' No, my grandfather wasn't willing, and so the name of Fox is not associated with Smith's crisps, alas.

Now what risks did Abraham take? Read Hebrews 11:8. In his commentary, F. F. Bruce calls this a 'mad adventure'; Abraham risked his security. He weighed up the choices. He probably said something like, 'Well, I could stay, it's safe here, Or I could go on this mad adventure into the unknown, grounded simply on God's bare word and promise.'

A classroom isn't a pulpit and you can do things there you couldn't do in front of a congregation. One of these things is what I call the 'chair test', in R.E. lessons. You get a youngster to come up to the front, and he stands on a chair with his back to the class and you say, 'Right. Now I am going to make you a promise.

Shut your eyes, fall off backwards and I will catch you.' So the little fellow falls over like a plank – most of them do it – and yours truly catches them. An act of faith on my bare word of promise. Actually the first time I did it I said, 'There! You've got faith. You believed me.' The boy said, 'No I didn't, I knew you'd catch me or you'd get into trouble.' But I tell you, if he hadn't had faith he'd still be standing on that chair. You've got to take risks. Why is it that so often the church is accused of being out of date and out of touch? Maybe it's because we're not prepared to take the mad adventure. We lean rather than learn. We like the security.

Another risk: Hebrews 11:17, 'By faith Abraham offered up Isaac . . . ' He risked his beloved only son. His whole life was bound up in Isaac. If there were no Isaac there would be no descendants, no nation. He was risking everything. Notice, Abraham never said, 'Let me die instead.' He took the hardest possible way. He sacrificed someone else on whom all his hopes rested. Every true sacrifice involves the risk of faith.

Remember Malachi, talking about those who offered lame animals to the Lord? I wonder if they thought, 'Well, God, you can have this lame one, but really, you can't have my best. All my future lies bound up in that one.'

Why was Abraham able to take such risks? I'll tell you why. It's in Romans 4:20; 'He grew strong in his faith as he gave glory to God.' He listened to God's word of promise. He meditated on God, and praised God. And so after forty years he was ready to risk everything for God.

And what sort of God was it that Abraham was trusting? Romans 4:17; 'The God who gives life to the dead', and verse 21: 'The God who is able to do what he has promised'.

3. *Abraham's faith kept him looking forward.* Like the apostle Paul, he kept pressing on. He had unconquerable hope. Inseparable twins: faith and hope. What were Abraham's hopes? He hoped for descendants, and he hoped for a land. It all seemed pretty unlikely. But, Romans 4:18; 'In hope he believed against hope.'

And you know, at ninety-nine years old, still hoping, this childless man accepts a change of name. From Abram – 'exalted father' – to Abraham – 'father of multitudes'. Isn't that lovely? Abraham had hope in a wonderful God.

He didn't only hope for descendants and a land. He hoped for a city (Hebrews 11:10). It's the heavenly city, the New Jerusalem. I wonder whether Abraham ever stood on the Mount of Olives and looked at the site of Solomon's temple. It wasn't going to be built for hundreds of years but I wonder if he ever looked at the site. I stood there recently and saw what I think must be the most beautiful view in the world – the city of Jerusalem. And yet behind that earthly city lies an invisible reality, the New Jerusalem. In Hebrews 12:22 it's 'the city of the living God'. The heavenly Jerusalem. Here's the truth to cheer a flagging heart. 'We have an inheritance in that city, an inheritance which is imperishable, undefiled and unfading.' We have a forward look. We have a great hope lying ahead of us. One of my Bible teachers was the late Alan Stibbs, and he used to say that the older he got and the nearer he got to heaven and the nearer to his death, the more he thought of heaven. Maybe we all need to do a lot more thinking about heaven.

I said we were going to study Abraham to be encouraged not by his faith but by the God in whom he trusted. And in conclusion I just want us to see three things that Abraham did.

Throughout his life he looked back and he rested on God's spoken promises; thus *he took faith.*

Throughout his life he looked up and gave glory to the God of glory; thus *he took risks.*

Throughout his life he looked forward and rejoiced in the city that God was preparing for him, and so *he took heart.*

Brothers and sisters, Abraham's God is our God, and we can see him in the face of Jesus Christ.

THE TRANSFORMING CHRIST
(Luke 24: 13–27)

by the Rev. Theodore Williams

We often sing a chorus: 'He lives, he lives, Christ Jesus lives today . . . You ask me how I know he lives; he lives within my heart.' Yes, the fact that Christ is alive is not a mere theological truth. It is an experience of reality. Someone has said that the reason the early Christians believed in the resurrection of Christ was not that they could not find the dead body of Christ, but that they found a living Christ. And on this day, the first day of the week, we are more conscious than ever before that Christ lives.

A Muslim once told a Christian missionary very scornfully, 'We have a proper tomb to show, but you have nothing.' That is the glory of it, is it not? We do not have a closed tomb to show but we can point to a living Christ. He lives. And he meets people along the corridors of life when they do not expect him to do so. That is as it was in the New Testament. We read about ten appearances of the risen Christ, and in many of these you will find he met people in times of need. He met Thomas in his gloom and doubt. He met Peter in

174

his back-sliding and failure. He met Mary Magdalene in her fear and confusion. He met Paul in his rebellion and disobedience.

What about these two disciples, the ones that were walking that distance of seven and a half miles from Jerusalem to Emmaus? They too were needy. The Bible does not say very clearly who they were. Perhaps they were of the greater circle of disciples whom our Lord had; besides the twelve who were his immediate disciples there were many others. And those two there on that road to Emmaus were in great need. We note first of all that their hearts were sad. You notice in verse 17, in the last part, they stood still, looking sad. They were sad, and the sadness that was in their hearts was reflected on their faces. They looked sad because their hearts were sad.

What was the reason for their sadness? Verse 21: 'We had hoped that he was the One to redeem Israel ... And besides all this it is now the third day since this happened.' They thought about the past. Yes, there are some people who have only a past to talk about and there is no future to think about. They said they had hoped in the Messiah, but now they stood with all their hopes and their expectations crushed. They were in deep despair, disappointed, disillusioned.

Why was it that they were sad? They did not know that Jesus Christ was to come and was to be crucified and was to rise again. They did not know that they believed in a God who was Sovereign God, who was in control of their circumstances. They did not understand God's purposes. Is this not the reason why we are sometimes confused and sad too? We do not understand that our God is sovereign. We do not grasp the fact that he has the control of our circumstances. Sometimes we have certain moulds into which we want to fit him, and when he does not fit into those moulds we too are confused and sad.

I remember talking to a young girl, a student in one of our medical colleges, a few years ago; and she said 'I do not believe that God loves, and it is very hard for me to pray any more and to have faith in God any more.' I asked her why. She said, 'Well, it is like this. I was expecting a letter from my boy friend and I did not get that letter. Then I started praying, and I said to God, "Now God, you must somehow get that letter to me." And it did not come. Then I said, "Now God, I will give you a week, let that letter come on this day." The letter never came. I said, "God, I will give you ten days." It never came. Now God does not answer prayer. He does not care for my feelings. Why did he allow this?' And I had to tell her: 'You have been using God, and now he is wanting to tell you, "Stop using me and start trusting me. Let me use you, let me have control of you." '

Yes; there are times when we begin to use God, when we want him to work according to our pattern and we want to fit him into our mould. And a sovereign God says, 'Let me be God, stop using me; I want to have control of your life instead of your controlling me and using me as a tool. I want you to be the instrument of my purposes.' And then we find that when things do not work as we have expected them to work we are disappointed, we are sad. What collapses is not God's purposes. What comes crashing down is not God in his sovereignty but it is your, and my, understanding of God. And then we say, 'Why did this happen?'

Sometimes we worship the God of our experience instead of experiencing the God of our worship. What do I mean by that? We say: 'Now I have experienced God

in this way all of these years, and this is the way he has
to work; because this is the way he has worked in the
past.' Is God committed to working only in one way all
the time in your life and mine? Just because he has
done a certain thing in a certain way in the past year, is
he committed to doing the same thing in the same way
this year? Let him be God. Let him be sovereign. Let
his purposes go forward. And sometimes, because we
have not grasped his purposes, because we have not
committed ourselves totally to a sovereign God, then
our hopes come crashing down. We talk about him in the
past tense and we have no hope in him for the future.

Now that was why they were sad. They said: 'We had
hoped that He was the One to redeem Israel, but now
all our hopes have come crashing down.' To be in the
place of sadness is not very healthy, because the place
of sadness is a very vulnerable place. It can very soon
become the place of failure. A man of God said, 'When
God's people get down in the dumps, Satan has them
defeated.' If we do not watch out, the place of sadness is
a place where we may be led into defeat and failure. Very
often a sadness or a disappointment that has come in, a
disillusionment that has come, leads us to depression
and failure. Is it wrong to be sad? We are human and
we are open to human emotions, and we may feel sad;
but then to allow sadness to overwhelm us and to drown
us and to take us into defeat – that need not happen.

There are many dangers present, because at a time of
sadness you are open to so many attacks of Satan. A
young woman lost her husband in very tragic circumstances. She kept asking the question, 'Why did this
happen?' Very often, when things do not work out the
way we have expected them to work out, when there is
no healing for the sickness, when there is no answer

to that prayer, when there is no deliverance in that particular dilemma, we ask, 'Why?' Now she asked, 'Why did my husband die?' She became very bitter, and in her bitterness she started openly rebelling against God. She began having affairs with other men and gave in to many other wrong ways of life, and she went far away, drifting away from God. It can happen. There are those who would drown their sadness in ways of living that do not bring any glory to God. A time of sadness can become a time of failure.

It can also become a time of fruitlessness. Sadness and depression can lead to barrenness of life. I was talking to someone some time back who said God had rebuked him because he had allowed his burden for his daughter to lead him to a place of bondage. His daughter was becoming wayward, was drifting away from the Lord, and instead of taking the burden to him and committing it into his hands and asking him to work, he took it upon himself; and this began to eat into his spiritual life, day in and day out. He lost his joy, his interest in prayer, his interest in testifying; and had become so paralysed and put out of action that there was nothing that he was doing for his God, and God's Spirit had shown him that he should not have got into this place of inaction and fruitlessness. His sadness had got him into this. Yes, that can happen.

'They stood still, looking sad.' That is what the Word says here. It is not wrong to feel sad because you and I are human, but it is certainly wrong to allow the sadness to put you out of action. There are some men and women today in God's service who are being put out of action because of some disappointment, some failure, some disillusionment. Somewhere they have allowed sadness to overwhelm them and lead them to defeat and also lead them to barrenness, paralysed because of sadness. They allowed their sadness to drown them because they did not grasp the purposes of God.

But the wonderful thing today is that the living Christ, the risen Christ, meets us in such situations. Notice how he addressed them in verse 25: 'O foolish men, and slow of heart to believe all that the prophets have spoken!' Certainly they were foolish; certainly they were slow of heart to believe. But that did not keep the risen Christ from coming into their lives. How wonderful it is to realise that by myself I may be foolish, I may be sad, dull of understanding and may not have grasped the purposes of God; and yet that does not limit the living Christ. He comes into my life all the same. And that was how it was in this case.

He drew near and walked along, and they did not recognise him, even as he was travelling with them. All that he wanted now was an opening. We see that they began to pour out their hearts to him. In verse 19, he said to them, 'What things?'; and they said to him, 'Concerning Jesus of Nazareth who was a prophet mighty in deed and word before God and all the people, and how our chief priests and rulers delivered him up to be condemned to death and crucified him.'

Their sad hearts now became opened hearts, open to Christ. The wonderful thing that you and I can have is the privilege of opening our hearts to a living Christ who comes along life's pathway. And all that he says is, 'Will you let me into your thoughts; will you let me into your heart? You are sad, yes. You have not grasped the purposes of a sovereign God and you have not realised that he has control of your circumstances. Therefore you have come into disappointment, disillusionment. You have come into sadness and it has drowned you and you have been paralysed and put out of action, and I am here, I want to get into your life, I want to get into your thoughts.

Why, *that* is exactly what the living Christ is trying to do. He is wanting to have access into our lives and thoughts, and it is possible on a Sunday morning such as this with that brilliant sunshine outside, with everything that should cause us to sing, we are doing anything but singing. We are sad. But the question is, does the living Christ have access into my thoughts, into my emotions, into my life, into my personality. 'They opened their hearts to him.'

They began to talk to him and they began to tell him all about their disappointment. A man of God said, 'Tell Christ all that is in your heart, like one who unloads his pent-up feelings to a dear friend.' Blessed are they who attain such familiar, undeserved intercourse with Christ. Oh, to pour out our hearts to him, to open our hearts, and to let him see our disillusionments and our disappointments and our sadness.

Not only did they open their hearts to him, they also opened their hearts to his Word. What did he do? Verse 27: 'Beginning with Moses and all the prophets he interpreted to them in all the Scriptures the things concerning Himself.' They opened their hearts to him and they opened their hearts to his Word as he spoke, as he thought, as he interpreted Scripture. That is where the answer to our sadness is. There is nothing outside of Christ. All that we need and all that we want and all that would meet our need is in Christ, the all-sufficient Christ, for him to have access to our lives and for us to be open to him and his Word.

When you open your heart and your life to him, Christ does something. And so they opened their hearts to him;

and very soon there was a commitment that was needed on their part. They came to Emmaus, and it looked as though he was going away. He was passing by. You read this of Jesus on another occasion as well, when the boat in which the disciples were sailing did not make any progress, and they saw the Lord coming to them walking on water. They were afraid; they thought it was a ghost. Then he gave them the word of cheer, and then, you will notice, it looked as though he was passing by and they had to invite him into the boat. That invitation signifies a commitment.

They had to tell him, 'Lord, we have opened our hearts to you, we have opened our thoughts to you, we have invited you into our thoughts. But now come into our homes, come into our lives.' And that is exactly what he did. In verse 29 you will notice, 'They constrained him saying, "Stay with us for it is toward evening and the day is now far spent." ' So he went in to stay with them. And what did he do when he went in to stay with them? Verse 30: 'When he was at table with them he took the bread and blest and brake it and gave it to them, and their eyes were opened and they recognised him; and he vanished out of their sight.' They invited him to be a guest but soon he became the host. They invited him to say with them, to be at their table, but he took control and he took the bread and he blest it, he broke it, and he gave it to them. Is not that what Jesus does, the living Christ? You want him to come into your sadness, but he wants to come into your life. You want to invite him into your problems, but he wants to come and take control of your entire personality.

There are some of us who would say, 'Now, Jesus, deal with me at this point and no more.' And Jesus says, 'Those are not the terms on which I would deal with you, my child; I want to take control of you completely and I want to do in you what I purpose to do.' I remember talking to a brother who said he had a problem in his job; there were people who were against him and they did things in his office to make him uncomfortable. He had been praying about it. Why did not God answer his prayer? And then as we began parting the question was asked, 'You want the Lord to come into your particular problem and to deal with it. What about your life? Does he have access to your life? Does he have access to all of your life?' He is not merely a problem solver. Jesus Christ will not come merely at your beck and call to do what you want him to do. He will come on his own terms and his own terms are he comes as the Sovereign Lord to take control and to transform.

They invited him in and he became the host. Is this not what he says in Revelation 3:20? It is again the living Christ speaking in this passage. 'Behold I stand at the door and knock. If any man hears my voice and opens the door I will come in to him and eat with him and he with Me.' I will come in as an invited guest and I will become the Lord, the Master. Their sad hearts became open hearts and open hearts became committed hearts. And what happened? Verses 32, 35; their burdened hearts became burning hearts; their sad hearts became singing hearts; their gloomy hearts became glory-filled hearts. All because they opened their hearts to the living Christ and to his Word. And when they opened their hearts to him and to his living Word, he called for a commitment; and their hearts became certainly committed hearts.

I wonder if this is exactly what the living Christ wants to do with you? You have been paralysed and put out of action because of what has happened in the past and you have been constantly living on that past. There has only been a past to talk about and there has been no future to think about as far as you are concerned. And Christ wants to enter into your heart, into your emotions, into your experiences and into your very life; and, having entered, he wants to take control. And when he takes control he transforms, and a transforming Christ can make your burdened heart a burning heart. He can make your sad heart a singing heart. He can make your gloomy heart a glory-filled heart. Glory be to Him.

MOVING MOUNTAINS
(Mark 11:12–27)

by the Rev. Ronald Dunn

I have some good news for you today and the good news is this: there is nothing wrong with you that a miracle wouldn't cure! If you're like most people you are saying, well, that's exactly what it *would* take; a miracle. There is no problem that you are wrestling with tonight, that a miracle wouldn't cure. 'But that's the trouble with miracles, there's never one around when you need it ...'

I think a great many Christians today have ceased to expect God to work in a miraculous way. We're like Peter when he saw the withered fig tree. He was amazed: 'Look, the fig tree which you cursed is withered!' I suppose he expected the Lord to be surprised too, the way he sounded. And I'm afraid that a great many of us don't really expect God to work miraculously, and if he should do so we would be utterly amazed – and expect God to be amazed also.

After I had been in the active pastorate for a while, years ago, I was reading through the book of Hebrews in the early hours of the morning and I came to the eleventh chapter, particularly those verses at the end where the writer really gets going. You know, where he's penning all the miraculous things that God has done through faith. And a little voice said, 'Well, you don't need to expect God to work like that today, after all, this is the twentieth century. God doesn't work that way any longer.' It wasn't the first time I had heard that voice and this time I spoke back to it. I said, 'Where did I ever get that idea?' And I said to myself, I am going to start reading the Bible again. If I can find anything in it that says that, then I am not going to believe in it any longer. And I have to tell you that I have yet to find anything in this book that tells me God has stopped working in a miraculous way. In fact everything I find seems to say that he is the same God, and he changes not.

And as Peter said, 'Lord, look at that,' the response of the Lord is almost as if he were saying, 'Now Peter, don't get excited, just have faith in God. Withering fig trees is nothing; if you know how to exercise faith in me you can do far more than that.' In fact Matthew, recording the same incident, says 'Jesus answered and said to them, "Truly I say to you, if you have faith and do not doubt, you shall not only do what was done to the fig tree, but even if you say to this mountain, be taken up and cast into the sea, it shall happen." '

Now I don't know about you, but I would have been satisfied with just withering fig trees. It seems there's a few fig trees around I'd like to wither. But the Lord is never stingy with his promises. He always does abundantly above all that we ask. I believe that Jesus is saying that if we know how to believe God, if we know how to trust him, we will see miracles of God in our day.

Now what do we mean by the word 'miracle'? It's bandied around a lot today and there are some extreme definitions. But let me give you mine. I believe very simply that a miracle is God doing something that only God can do. And isn't that what we need today?

Another thing we need to examine: what is a 'mountain'? Well, I don't believe that Jesus actually meant us to go around moving mountains. After all, given enough dynamite a man can do that himself. No, over and over in the Bible you will see that mountains symbolise barriers, hindrances, obstacles. And I think that what Jesus means by a mountain is anything that is standing in our path, hindering us from doing God's will; when the world, the flesh or the devil throws something in my path and says stop, this is as far as you can go. And I think he is saying that if you and I know how to believe God there is nothing that can stop us from doing what God wants us to do. Isn't that good news?

So I want to examine tonight this mountain-moving faith, and there are three things I would suggest to you out of this passage.

1. *This kind of power is released only by faith.* There is in Matthew 17 almost a parallel to the incident here. It's after the Mount of Transfiguration. The Lord was returning with James, John and Peter. Out of the crowd came a father whose son was possessed by a demon. Now in Matthew 10:28, Jesus gave the disciples power to cast out demons. But they were unable to cast out this demon, and when Jesus returned the father came to Jesus and said, 'Master, I brought my sick boy to your disciples but they could not cure him.' Those are sad words. The tragedy isn't the demon-possessed boy, but the powerless disciples. Jesus showed his impatience, and then with a word restored that boy to normality.

Then, the Bible says, the disciples came to Jesus privately. I don't blame them. They must have been absolutely humiliated. They'd all had a try at it and were puzzled and embarrassed and humiliated, and they came to Jesus privately. And they asked him a good question. 'Lord, why could we not cast him out?'

What they were really asking was, 'Lord, why can't we do what you have promised we could do?' Have you ever asked that question? It's a good question. What did Jesus answer?

I was amazed recently to find a popular commentary which said that the reason the disciples could not cast out the demon was that they did not realise that the gift was temporary. Now, I don't want to enter into the question of temporary and non-temporary gifts, but the issue is settled by what Jesus himself said. 'Because of the littleness of your faith. Because of your unbelief.'

Did you know that God allows us to set the limit and level of our own blessings? He does! It is 'according to our faith', and Jesus said, 'Have faith in God.' The Greek, notice, put 'God' in the 'emphatic position', which means that the emphasis belongs to God. The emphasis is on God, not faith. And it is very significant that Jesus' emphasis is not on faith but its object.

I think a great many of us worry about the size of our faith. There's a verse going around the States, 'Have faith in faith.' Well, the only thing wrong with that is, it's wrong. The Bible never tells us to have faith in faith, because ultimately that means having faith in yourself. When we are confronted with some obstacle most of us take out our faith and look at it and measure it and the conclusion we come to is, it's too small and weak. One of the things I found, however, when I read the Gospels with an eye on this matter is that everyone

187

who came to Jesus for help, – with two exceptions – came with a weak and imperfect faith. And yet Jesus still met their need. Spurgeon said, 'Don't make a Christ of your faith.' It's not faith that saves but Christ.

Let me illustrate it like this. Several years ago we went walking round some frozen lakes in Colorado. One of my friends said, 'Preacher, get out there and walk on that lake – maybe your only chance to walk on water.' I refused. He said, 'I skate on these all winter long, they will hold you, they're solid. Go on.' Well, I ventured after a while, about three feet out, kind of tip-toed, looking for cracks, didn't put all my weight down. And then in the car on the way back I looked out of the window and saw a man sitting on a wooden crate in the middle of one of these frozen lakes. He had got a hole in the lake and was fishing. Now, that man's faith was such that it got not only him but a wooden crate as well out to the middle of the lake. My faith was so weak I would only venture out three feet. Now, which of us was the safer? Was he safer than I was? No. You see, if it had been faith holding us up I'd have sunk immediately. But it wasn't. It was the ice holding us up.

You ask, then, what is the point of having a great faith over a little faith? Ah, I'm glad you ask. The advantage of the great faith was that it enabled that man to launch into the middle of the ice and enjoy what he was doing. I was nervous all the time. That's the difference. The person with great faith is not afraid to get out into the middle of God's will and enjoy what he is doing. The person with weak faith is always nervous, always looking for cracks in the ice.

Well, as we drove away, I said to the driver, 'Wonder where he got all that faith?' I'll never forget the answer: 'Oh, he lives round here. He knows the ice.' Do you know where great faith comes from? From knowing the Lord. And the greater your knowledge of the Lord Jesus Christ, the greater your faith will be. So this is the first thing. This kind of power is released only by faith.

2. *This kind of faith is expressed by prayer.* Look at verse 24: 'Therefore I say to you' – and Jesus is tying the two together, making a practical application – 'all things for which you pray and ask, believe that you have received them and they shall be granted you.'

You want to move a mountain? Faith, faith in God. How is this faith to be expressed? By believing prayer. Tell me about your prayer life and I'll tell you about the mountains that you are moving.

If the president of my bank wrote me a letter and said, 'Preacher, anything you need, don't worry about it; just call me on the phone' – he'd have to install a telephone line, I'd call him so much. If I didn't, what would it mean? It would mean that I didn't take him at his word. This kind of faith is expressed in prayer.

3. *This kind of praying is regulated by forgiveness.* Look at verse 25. Notice that the little word 'and' tells us that this is a continuation and a completion. Jesus starts out by talking about moving mountains. How do you do it? By faith. How do you express that faith? By praying. How do you pray? 'When you stand praying, if you have aught against anybody, forgive.' Isn't that amazing? I mean, what does forgiveness have to do with moving mountains? Why does the Lord bring up such an unpleasant subject when we were enjoying talking about faith and prayer?

I believe that the greatest cause of unanswered prayer is an unforgiving spirit among God's people. And I believe we could take it back to this. If I am not moving mountains in my life, if the will of God has been brought

189

to a halt in my life, I believe that the first place to look
for the cause is my relationship with my fellow men.

I was reading a moment ago in Matthew 7. You have
there (verse 11) another tremendous prayer promise.
'If ye then being evil know how to give good gifts to
your children, how much more shall your Father who
is in heaven give what is good to those who ask them.'
Verse 12, 'Therefore' – tying it together – 'whatever you
want others to do for you do so for them, for this is the
law and the prophets.'

Now that is what I call the Golden Rule. For years I
read it like this: 'Whatever I don't want people to do to
me, I must not do to them.' That's not what Jesus says.
That's strictly negative. No, it is a positive statement.
You see? I am praying that God will give me good
things, and he says, 'All right, while you're praying to
God for good things I want you in turn to express the
spirit and nature of your heavenly Father and give good
things to those who need them.' You see – again our
Lord connects the two things together. Our prayer
life is conditioned by our relationships with our fellow
men.

It says, 'If ye have aught against any, forgive.' Not
'if they apologise', not 'if they promise not to do it
again'. 'If ye have aught against any, forgive.'

Do you know why you were able to repent, yourself,
in the first place? It is because forgiveness had already
been provided by God in his grace and mercy through
the sacrifice of the Lord Jesus. What does it mean to
forgive? Not to 'forgive and forget'. Only the Lord
has the ability to forget. You will not be able to forget,
but that's a greater testimony to the grace of God in
your heart. 'I remember he did it, but I forgive him. It's
no longer an issue, it doesn't matter.' Let me illustrate.

We all of us, whether we know it or not, carry a little black book around with us. In it we keep all the 'I.O.U.'s' we're holding against people. You know how it is. 'I'm holding an I.O.U. against Mrs Jones for what she said about me.' 'I'm holding an I.O.U. against the pastor because he didn't call on me.' You know what forgiveness is? It's tearing those I.O.U.'s up and saying, 'They don't owe me a thing. They may have wronged me, they may have harmed me, but I forgive, I forgive, I forgive.' If you have faith, you can move mountains.

May I close with a question. Is it possible that there is a mountain facing us that we have been unable to remove because we are hanging on to one little I.O.U. against somebody? Isn't it worth seeing that mountain cast into the sea? Just tear up that I.O.U. This kind of power is released only by faith. This kind of faith is expressed only by prayer. This kind of prayer is conditioned by forgiveness.

KESWICK CONVENTION 1978

Tape list of addresses included in this book:

Rev. John Stott Bible Readings:

Rev. Dick Lucas Bible Readings:

These tapes can be obtained, together with a full list of Keswick tapes, from:

Anthony C. Gill, Tape Secretary,
Keswick Convention Tape Library,
13 Lismore Road,
Eastbourne,
East Sussex BN21 3BA.